Bloom's
GUIDES

J.D. Salinger's
The Catcher in the Rye

CURRENTLY AVAILABLE

The Adventures of Huckleberry Finn
All the Pretty Horses
Animal Farm
Beloved
Brave New World
The Catcher in the Rye
The Chosen
The Crucible
Cry, the Beloved Country
Death of a Salesman
Fahrenheit 451
The Glass Menagerie
The Grapes of Wrath
Great Expectations
The Great Gatsby
Hamlet
The Handmaid's Tale
The House on Mango Street
I Know Why the Caged Bird Sings
The Iliad
Lord of the Flies
Macbeth
Maggie: A Girl of the Streets
The Member of the Wedding
The Metamorphosis
Of Mice and Men
1984
The Odyssey
One Hundred Years of Solitude
Pride and Prejudice
Ragtime
Romeo and Juliet
Slaughterhouse-Five
The Scarlet Letter
Snow Falling on Cedars
A Streetcar Named Desire
A Tale of Two Cities
The Things They Carried
To Kill a Mockingbird

Bloom's
GUIDES

J.D. Salinger's
The Catcher in the Rye

Edited & with an Introduction
by Harold Bloom

CHELSEA HOUSE
PUBLISHERS
An imprint of Infobase Publishing

Bloom's Guides: The Catcher in the Rye

Copyright © 2007 by Infobase Publishing
Introduction © 2007 by Harold Bloom

Chelsea House
An imprint of Infobase Publishing
132 West 31st Street
New York NY 10001

Library of Congress Cataloging-in-Publication Data
J.D. Salinger's The catcher in the rye / [edited by] Harold Bloom.
   p. cm. — (Bloom's guides)
 Includes bibliographical references and index.
 ISBN 0-7910-9296-8
 1. Salinger, J. D. (Jerome David), 1919- Catcher in the rye—
Examinations—Study guides. 2. Salinger, J. D. (Jerome David), 1919—-
Criticism and interpretation. I. Bloom, Harold. II. Title: Catcher in the rye. III. Series.

 PS3537.A426C329 2007
 813'.54—dc22   2006031070

Contributing Editor: Janyce Marson

Cover design by Takeshi Takahashi

Printed in the United States of America

Bang EJB 10 9 8 7 6 5 4 3 2 1

This book is printed on acid-free paper.

Contents

Introduction

HAROLD BLOOM

The Catcher in the Rye is frequently compared to Mark Twain's *Adventures of Huckleberry Finn*, a dangerous comparison for Salinger's book, since Twain's work stands with Herman Melville's *Moby-Dick*, Walt Whitman's *Leaves of Grass*, Nathaniel Hawthorne's *The Scarlet Letter*, and Emily Dickinson's poetry as one of the handful of essential American books. Yet the link between Huck Finn and Holden Caulfield is palpable; Holden is necessarily one of the modern American descendants of Huck, for Huck there is still the frontier; he always can light out for the territory. Holden only has mid-century Manhattan, which will not provide him with the big river, Jim, and the raft. Alas, Manhattan gives Holden nothing positive; as many readers have noted, the city is his descent into Hell. Still, this may have more to do with Holden than with Manhattan. Like Huck, Holden is a boy of endless good will, but he is considerably less healthy than Huck, who is not a masochist. Holden is, and there is an element of doom-eagerness in his Manhattan adventures. Ambivalence, the simultaneous presence of positive and negative feelings in almost equal degree, dominates Holden throughout the book, in regard to his father, and to the entire adult world, but also to his own self.

We know Holden primarily as a narrative voice, which is the way we know Huck. Between Huck and Holden the clearest mediating figure is Nick Carraway, who narrates Scott Fitzgerald's *The Great Gatsby*. Carraway is a grownup who still shares in an adolescent's sensibility, and his admiration for Gatsby's greatness is echoed by Holden. Voice, properly modulated by a master storyteller, can tell us everything we need to know about a literary character, and there are few mysteries in Holden for the attentive reader. This is impressive because Salinger does not provide Holden with a very long foreground: hate we learn, we learn directly by listening to Holden. He has lost his younger brother Allie to sickness and to death, and he is haunted by the loss: it is not too much to say that he is traumatized by it. Thirteen when Allie died, Holden is seventeen at the time of the novel, but his emotions remain arrested, as though he cannot grow older than he was then. Holden is a depressive who desperately needs help, but is too oppositional to seek it out. He suffers also from the guilt of a survivor, irrational guilt but immensely compelling.

And yet Holden, a vital and potentially strong consciousness, is considerably more than his illness, and is not to be regarded as a clinical study. He lacks the sturdiness of Huck Finn's spirit, and Huck's mythological largeness, but he has a spiritual eminence that is all his own. Distrusting all language, his own as much as any, he nevertheless has a faith in goodness and in love that invests him with authentic pathos. He will always remain vulnerable, but that is the cost of his confirmation as a kind of alienated saint, whose deepest wish is to be savior of children. Despite his sufferings, Holden remains an image of freedom, which is his most authentic inheritance from Huck Finn. Unlike Huck, who learns from Jim and from shrewdly observing everyone he encounters (except the tiresome Tom Sawyer), Holden scarcely is able to learn anything in the course of his book, because he cannot invest his trust in anyone who is not an image of innocence and he knows that only the dead and the very young are innocent. That makes survival very difficult for Holden, as he has no guides or teachers whom he can accept. And yet Holden does have a Huck-like genius for survival, despite his depressive doom-eagerness. At the end, lovingly watching his sister while the healing rain falls upon him, Holden becomes a figure of capable poignance, and persuades us implicitly that he will survive for some larger end or purpose, benign and generous in a more organized version of innocence.

Biographical Sketch

Of the relatively scant information regarding his personal life, J.D. Salinger is best known for not wanting to be famous. He lives today in rural New Hampshire, shunning all public attention. Indeed, seclusion is Salinger's preferred way of life and, accordingly, he has been reticent in talking about himself or his work. Yet, his reticence notwithstanding, Salinger's fiction displays a remarkable empathy for the individual, expressive power of speech, most especially through the voice of children and adolescents, a focus which places him squarely in the American literary tradition with such writers as Mark Twain, Ring Lardner and Ernest Hemingway, to name just a few.

Jerome David Salinger was born in the fashionable apartment district of Manhattan on January 1, 1919, the second child of Sol, a prosperous Jewish importer and Marie Jillich, of Scots-Irish descent, who changed her name to Miriam when she married Sol. His only sibling, a sister, Doris, was born eight years before him. Between 1932 and 1934, he attended the McBurney School, in Manhattan, but did not complete his studies there. In 1936, he graduated from Valley Forge Military Academy, in Wayne, Pennsylvania, near Philadelphia, where he served as literary editor of *Crossed Sabres*, the school yearbook. Some critics claim that his years at Valley Forge were the source for some of the material in *The Catcher in the Rye*. However, though some similarities exist, the connections between the novel and his own school days remain at best superficial, despite his comments to the contrary that his childhood was very much like that of his protagonist, Holden Caulfield.

In 1937, Salinger visited Vienna and Poland with his father, reputedly to learn the family importing business. Upon his return in 1938, Salinger briefly attended Ursinus College in Pennsylvania where he wrote a column, "Skipped Diploma," which featured movie reviews for the college newspaper. Following his brief tenure at Ursinus, Salinger enrolled in a course in short-story writing a Columbia University taught by Whit Burnett, then editor of *Story* magazine. According to Paul Alexander,[2] Salinger spent most of the first semester in the back of the class, contributing very little. However, sometime during the end of the fall semester Salinger became animated and engaged and turned in three short stories, which made a profound impression on Whit Burnett. Salinger's first published story, "The Young Folks," appeared in 1940, in *Story*, for which he was paid twenty-five dollars, and "Go See Eddie" in the *University of Kansas City Review* following its rejection by *Esquire*. His literary success continued in 1941 with the publication of "The Hang of It" in *Collier's*, followed by the sale of "The Heart of a Broken Story" to *Esquire* in November of 1941, although the publication of the latter was delayed until 1946 due to the United States entry into World War II. Salinger was likewise called into service and was classified 1-B by Selective Service, working on the M.S. *Kungsholm* as entertainment director.

In 1942, at the beginning of the Second World War, Salinger was reclassified by Selective Service and drafted into the U.S. Army. He attended the Officers, First Sergeants, and Instructors School of the Signal Corps and was later transferred to the Army Counterintelligence Corps. During the year, Salinger published "The Long Debut of Lois Taggett" in *Story* and "Personal Notes of an Infantryman" in *Colliers*. During this year, Salinger corresponded with Oona O'Neill, the daughter of playwright Eugene O'Neill and, later, Charlie Chaplin's wife. In 1943, while stationed in Nashville, Tennessee, he published "The Varioni Brothers" in the *Saturday Evening Post*. Later in the year, he was transferred to the Army CounterIntelligence Corps and received training at Tiverton in Devonshire, England. On June 6, 1944, Salinger participated in the Normandy invasion—known as D-Day— and came ashore at Utah Beach with the Fourth Division. Salinger would write much throughout the war years. Later, while stationed in Europe, he was security agent for the Twelfth Infantry Regiment, which marched to Paris through treacherous roads and arrived there on August 25. Once in

Paris, Salinger found time to visit Ernest Hemingway, who at the time was himself working as a war correspondent. According to his daughter, Margaret Salinger, her father's visit with Hemingway was a warm one, with Hemingway stating his appreciation for the story, "The Last Day of the Last Furlough."[1]

Following his brief stay in Paris, Salinger's regiment crossed into Germany, arriving on September 12. His story, "A Boy in France," expresses a soldier's exhaustion with the journey. Once in Germany, his regiment endured a winter of unspeakable conditions in the frozen Hürtgen Forest which sustained an enormous number of casualties. Margaret writes that her father told her he would always be grateful for the knitted socks his mother mailed to him, stating that they saved his life in the foxholes. She continues to say that his story, "For Esmé," which "falls silent when it does," evidences the incomplete recovery of language when expressing such extreme experiences as World War II. On May 5, 1945, the Twelfth Regiment opened a command post in Herman Göring's castle at Neuhaus, and carried out its occupation duties. In his capacity as counterintelligence officer, Salinger and his fellow officers had the task of maintaining security amidst a throng of displaced persons, Allied prisoners of war and German political prisoners. Sometime in July, Salinger was hospitalized in Germany for what has been described as battle fatigue or a minor breakdown. As his daughter explains, he wrote a letter to Hemingway, making light of his war experiences, but emphatically stating that he absolutely would not submit to a psychiatric evaluation. She is also of the opinion that the trauma of her father's wartime experiences is to be found in *The Catcher in Rye* where Nazis are displaced as "phonies" and those in positions of authority, such as professors dressed in "tweeds," have an equally devastating effect on the emotional lives of the people for whom they are responsible. Though the battlefield is gone, Holden nevertheless calls out for his dead brother, Allie, and is in an equally desperate fight for his life and a way to reconnect with people. During this same year, Salinger published other short stories—"Elaine," "This Sandwich Has

No Mayonnaise" and "I'm Crazy," the latter being the first published story to introduce material used in *The Catcher in the Rye*.

When the war ended in 1945, Salinger was discharged from the Army. He was married, briefly, to a French woman named Sylvia, a doctor, whom Salinger had at first arrested and interrogated. Little is known about her due to Salinger's relentless determination to prevent information about his life from ever entering the public domain. However, Salinger's daughter provides some interesting details about her father's opinion of Sylvia, namely that she was passionate but evil, a woman who "bewitched" him. Their marriage was very short-lived with the couple being divorced in 1946. Back in New York, Salinger began to spend a lot of time enjoying the nightlife of Greenwich Village in the company of aspiring writers and actors, and began to study Zen Buddhism, which would become a central part of his life in years to come. From this time on, Salinger's stories were appearing in print regularly, most often in *The New Yorker*. "A Perfect Day for Bananafish," published during this period, first introduces the character Seymour Glass, who appears later in "Seymour: An Introduction." Darryl F. Zanuck, a producer at 20th Century-Fox, acquired the rights to "Uncle Wiggily in Connecticut," another story that was published in *The New Yorker*, and in 1949 was made *My Foolish Heart*, starring Susan Hayward. In fact, Hayward was nominated for an Academy Award for her role as Eloise; the film, however, had little to do with Salinger's story.

In 1950, *The New Yorker* published Salinger's "For Esmé—with Love and Squalor," to favorable reviews. By now, Salinger had acquired a reputation as a writer of short fiction. He received an offer from Harcourt Brace, in New York, to publish *The Catcher in the Rye*, but withdrew his manuscript when he encountered problems with the editorial staff; it was published the following year by Little, Brown. The novel won critical and popular acclaim and was on *The New York Times* best-seller list for seven months. Salinger wanted desperately to maintain his privacy, but the success of his book was forcing the creator of Holden Caulfield reluctantly into the limelight.

To escape publicity, in 1953, Salinger moved to Cornish, New Hampshire following a visit he made with his sister, Doris, during a beautiful Indian summer in the fall of 1952. They had with them some pocket money from the publication of *The Catcher* and were in search of a place where Salinger could write without the distractions of the city. During their drive through New England, they fell in love with Cape Ann, an area north of Boston, but found they could not afford the real estate prices. When they arrived in Cornish, they found the landscape spectacular, but the house for sale a disaster with no running water, no bathroom facilities, a hovel of a kitchen and a two-storied living room with exposed beams that resembled a barn, complemented by a large family of squirrels that had taken up residence in the rafters. When Salinger bought the house, Doris remembered Holden's fantasy of living in the woods.

> ... "I'd build me a little cabin somewhere with the dough I made and live there for the rest of my life.... I'd meet this beautiful girl that was also a deaf-mute and we'd get married.... If we had any children we'd hide them somewhere. We could buy them a lot of books and teach them how to read and write by ourselves."

Jerome Salinger would move into this house on New Year's Day, 1953, on his thirty-fourth birthday, where he would later spend many long weekends with Claire Douglas and whom he would later marry.

As Claire was still in college at Radcliffe and needed written permission from a respectable person in order to be away from college for the weekend, the couple composed some fictitious letters from a hostess named "Mrs. Trowbridge," describing Claire's lovely visits at the winter cottage. Salinger asked Claire to drop out of school and live with him in Cornish. When Claire refused to do this, Salinger dropped out of sight, which precipitated her collapse and long bout with mononucleosis and an appendectomy. Salinger eventually reappeared in her life during the summer of 1954 and by the fall Claire had moved in with him. As she was still completing her coursework at Radcliffe, Claire and J.D. spent Tuesday through Thursday of each week in Cambridge, Massachusetts where, due to issues of propriety, Salinger took a room at the Commodore Hotel, while Claire shared an apartment with five other divorced women. Salinger was very unhappy with this arrangement and the interruption of his work. Claire eventually dropped out of college, just four months before graduation. On February 17, 1955 Claire Douglas married Jerome Salinger.

Their marriage, however, was not a fairytale. Though they saw friends in New York and Boston, the couple became thoroughly isolated in Cornish, New Hampshire once Claire became pregnant with their first child, Margaret. Claire had even gone so far as to burn the papers she wrote in college, including some fictional pieces. For his part, Salinger worked sixteen hours a day, searching for a philosophy of life to live by, and began eating only organically-grown food prepared in special types of cooking oils—a diet that Claire was not at all interested in. Indeed, she became resentful. Their daughter, Margaret Ann, was born on December 10, 1955; their son, Matthew, was born on February 13, 1960. In 1967, the Salingers were divorced.

Salinger continued to publish fiction from his self-enforced isolation in New Hampshire. When *Franny and Zooey*, which appeared as separate short stories in *The New Yorker*, was published in book form by Little, Brown in 1961, it was an immediate success. Two other stores, "Raise High the Roof Beam, Carpenters" and "Seymour: An Introduction," also appearing first in *The New Yorker*, were published in book form in 1963. Salinger's last published short story, "Hapworth 16, 1924," an epistolary novella in the form of a long letter from seven-year old Seymour Glass from summer camp, appeared in *The New Yorker* on June 19, 1965 and was published in book form in 1998. Except for denouncing *The Complete Short Stories of J.D. Salinger*, which contains the stories that were published in magazines other than *The New Yorker*, in 1974, and for suing

Ian Hamilton and Random House for publishing his unauthorized biography, in 1987, J.D. Salinger remains a virtual recluse.

Notes
1. Salinger, Margaret. *Dream Catcher: A Memoir*. New York: Washington Square Press, 2000.
2. Alexander, Paul. *Salinger: A Biography*. Los Angeles: Renaissance Books, 1999.

The Story Behind the Story

Censorship and *The Catcher in the Rye*

The history of the reception of *The Catcher in the Rye* by various institutions and segments of society is equally as contentious as the odyssey of its rebellious protagonist, Holden Caulfield. A novel which is a period piece about life in post-World War II America, *The Catcher in the Rye* has been branded as anti-religious, unpatriotic (especially within the context of the McCarthy era), and immoral and obscene in its treatment of sexual themes and its use of profane and slang language. The antidote for this "perceived" menace would be censorship and, accordingly, shortly after it's publication in 1951, *The Catcher in the Rye* met with vehement opposition by certain social organizations and special interest groups in the United States. What follows is a brief overview of a few of the more salient instances in the novel's struggle to gain acceptance and, indeed, permission, to be read and discussed in schools, libraries and other public forums.

1954 saw the first attempts to censor the novel in Marin and Los Angeles counties, California, followed by eight more attempts across the nation in 1955-56 from sanctioned high school reading materials. In each of these initial attacks on *The Catcher in the Rye*, the attempt to have the novel banned was initiated by a parent or other "concerned citizen" because it was deemed dangerous for one or more of the above-mentioned reasons. During this time, the umbrella organization presiding over this form of censorship was the National Organization for Decent Literature (NODL), a group founded in 1938 by the Catholic Bishops of the United States and comprised of Catholic women active in their communities. Its agenda was to protect the morality of the United States. Initially, the NODL focused on the content of magazines and comic books, the literature read by adolescents. However, by the 1950s, the focus and *modus operandi* of the NODL had evolved with the times and the spotlight shifted to paperback books, most particularly those read in high school, as well as textbook material, the latter being monitored by textbook commissions within local school districts.

The social revolution of the 1960's notwithstanding, the effort to ban the novel by certain groups persisted. To be sure, during this time the American Association of University Professors and the American Library Association waged its own campaign against censorship, and, in subsequent decades, other groups would form to counter the advocates of censorship. Nevertheless, in 1968, a group of parents from Grosse Pointe, a sophisticated and affluent suburb of Detroit, initiated a campaign to remove the book, as did a similar group of twenty parents in Beloit, Wisconsin. The latter branded *Catcher* objectionable, and even launched an attack against *Romeo and Juliet*, referring to Shakespeare as "a dirty old man." One newspaper reported that "[p]arents will judge their books not on their literary value but on what they consider 'filth.'"

In 1972, an advisory board member of the Shawnee Mission Advisory Board responded to reports that there was an effort to ban the book from a sophomore literature class, stating that the *Kansas City Star* had misrepresented them in reporting on their meeting. Rather than conceding that censorship was at work, Mrs. Florence Dubois stated that the word "ban" had never been used and that it had never suggested that *Catcher in the Rye* be removed from libraries. This is, of course, exactly the kind of hypocrisy that Holden Caulfield would rail against.

In 1981, a debate ensued over whether *Catcher in the Rye* and other books should be banned from a North Carolina classroom, prompted by a request from pastor Randy Stone, who was concerned that the book took God's name in vain. Stone's objections were refuted by another member of the clergy, pastor Fred Ohler, who questioned why profanity and sexuality in Salinger and Steinbeck were more of a moral concern than poverty and adult hypocrisy. At the crux of this debate was the question as to whether Christian philosophy should prevail over "objectionable" literature. In fact, the seeds of this type of excoriation were sown by such men as Mr. Charles Keating, founder of an organization called "Citizens for Decent Literature" in 1958, and publisher of *The National Decency Reporter*, who in 1962 won the praise of *Reader's Digest*, which described him as an all-American boy possessing the qualities necessary to lead the vanguard against indecent literature.

Indeed, attempts to ban *Catcher in the Rye* from various high school curriculums, booksellers and school libraries would continue though the 1990s, although it remained enormously popular and had a large group of critics and other advocates that extolled its many virtues. Perhaps one of best examples of the book's positive influence is the instance in which a student cited the novel in defense of a student newspaper which was banned in a Pennsylvania high school. The student argued that the school newspaper should be allowed on the ground that *Catcher* was on the school's recommended reading list despite its obscene language and vulgarity. It is a foregone conclusion that Holden Caulfield would have felt tremendous pride in knowing that someone finally understood him and believed in his cause.

The Catcher in the Rye in the American Canon

In addition to creating a maelstrom of controversy in its critical reception, *The Catcher in Rye* has a great deal to tell us about the nature of J.D. Salinger's creativity and artistic achievement. Two important critical instances mentioned below concern the language of the novel and its unique place in the American literary canon: Donald P. Costello's discussion of *The Catcher's* linguistic significance and Pamela Hunt Steinle's discussion of the status of American Adam.

Donald Costello begins his discussion of *The Catcher's* use of the teenage vernacular in the 1950s by listing the many instances in which critics at the time of its publication found it to be "a true and authentic rendering of teenage colloquial speech" in addition to its daring use of profanity and the comic effect of those blasphemous statements.[1] Indeed, Costello's essay discusses the many ways in which Holden's use of language is typical. However, this general consensus notwithstanding, Costello maintains that J.D. Salinger's most important linguistic challenge was that of an artist seeking to "creat[e] an individual character, not with the linguistic task of reproducing the exact speech of teenagers in general" (172) but, rather, "a character with strong personal idiosyncrasies which in many ways expresses himself in the familiar teenage habits of speech and thought processes." Thus, while admitting that Holden's schoolboy obscenities, vulgarities and sloppy grammar are typical of the prep-school vernacular, Costello argues that Holden's individuality resides in his sensitivity and self-consciousness. Costello notes that Holden never swears or uses crude words in a phony way, but only as an expression of his emotional state. Most importantly, when addressing the reader directly, Holden's use of "forbidden" words is almost completely absent. He further points out that since Holden is both intelligent and well-read, much of his commentary and figures of speech reflect his education, thereby elevating his statements above the typical teenage vocabulary. Costello maintains that for Holden, communication is preeminent and his manner of speaking is always self-consciously motivated by a desire to convey his true feelings. Thus, evidence of Holden's true individuality resides in his very self-conscious use of language.

Pamela Hunt Steinle's discussion of the status of a "postwar American Fable" in *The Catcher in the Rye* takes up the issue of the novel's enduring appeal and why it has remained a "formative" book to be shared by different generations. Steinle argues that its status as a classic is to be found in Salinger's carefully wrought characterization of Holden Caulfield. Using R.W.B. Lewis's identification of a "native American mythology,"[2] "an authentic figure of heroic innocence and vast potentiality, posed at the start of a new history," found in nineteenth-century literature, and his positioning of *The Catcher in the Rye* as one of three post-World War II novels which continue in this tradition, albeit in a diminished form, Steinle locates the true source of cultural tension. What follows is only a brief summary of an important chapter in Steinle's book, "The Catcher in the Rye *as Postwar American Fable*,"[3] a vast and extremely important critical perspective important to an understanding of the novel's place within the American canon, and a topic which merits further reading and discussion.

Steinle uses Lewis's critique of an American Adam, a character "self reliant" and ready to confront his destiny, to show how Salinger's novel both partakes of this literary tradition and departs from it in the figure of Holden Caulfield, a diminished Adam who finds himself alone in an indifferent, and oftentimes hostile, environment. While citing such nineteenth-century classics as James Fenimore Cooper's *The Deerslayer*, with which *Catcher in the Rye* has been compared, Steinle sees the latter as implying a new mission for its Adamic hero, namely a pacifism except in the service of innocents. Steinle refers to such instances as Holden's bloody fight with Stradlater in an effort to protect the honor of a female friend and his recognition that he has lost that battle as an example of a new pacifism for the hero. Furthermore, she states that this new Adam must endure a reduction in status for he must now demonstrate an ability to survive an unfortunate fall from grace, which unhappy circumstance brings suffering, but can also provide the impetus for growth and moral understanding. For this, Steinle finds ample evidence in Holden's departure from Pencey Prep. Upon arriving in New York City, Holden must confront a wide variety of phonies, criminals and perverts as he moves from seedy hotels and bars, stale cabs, hotel pimps and prostitutes through his traumatic visit with Mr. Antolini, the last hope he had for moral support and nurturing. Steinle concludes that Holden is an absurd hero who emerges happy at the end of his journey.

Notes

1. Costello, Donald P. "The Language of *The Catcher in the Rye*." *American Speech* XXXIV (October 1959): 172–81. New York: Columbia University Press.

2. Lewis, R. W. B. *The American Adam: Innocence, Tragedy, and Tradition in the Nineteenth Century*. Chicago: University of Chicago Press, 1964.

3. Steinle, Pamela Hunt. *In Cold Fear: The Catcher in the Rye Censorship Controversies and Postwar American Character*. Columbus: Ohio State University Press, 2000.

List of Characters

Holden Caulfield is the sixteen year-old narrator whose experiences form the action of the novel. With a history of expulsion from and failure at various prep schools, his recent expulsion from Pencey Prep, and profound disappointment with the phony and hypocritical institutions in which he must maneuver, leads to an emotional breakdown.

Phoebe Caulfield is Holden's younger sister, whom he thoroughly loves and respects. Phoebe is ten, but very clever and sympathetic. However, towards the end of the novel, he is disappointed that Phoebe scolds him for being expelled from school and questions what he is going to do with his life. However, demonstrates her unconditional love for Holden in the end when she packs her suitcase and wants to run away with him.

Allie, Holden's younger brother, died of leukemia on July 18, 1946. Holden loves his brother and misses him profoundly. One of his fondest memories of Allie, and a recurring theme throughout the novel, is his fielder's mitt on which he had written poems all over in green ink. Holden keeps the fielder's mitt with him wherever he goes.

D.B. is Holden's older brother, a writer who once published a collection called "The Secret Goldfish" and is now employed as a scriptwriter in Hollywood.

Mr. and Mrs. Caulfield are Holden's parents. They are incapable of providing him with the parental understanding that he needs. Mr. Caulfield is a corporation lawyer, and Mrs. Caulfield is a housewife. Very little is revealed about his parents.

Mr. Antolini is Holden's English teacher from Elkton Hills who is now teaching at New York University. Holden holds him in the highest regard. However, when Holden decides to pay hin a visit in his hour of need, he is scared off by what he believes are Mr. Antolini's advances towards him, a fact that remains very ambiguous.

Mrs. Antolini, Mr. Antolini's wife, is both more wealthy and older than her husband.

Jane Gallagher is Holden's childhood friend. Though they never actually dated, they used to hold hands. Jane is best remembered by Holden for the way she used to keep all her kings in the back row during checkers. She is never actually present in a scene, but is constantly in Holden's thoughts and memories. Holden seems to feel tremendous respect and affection for Jane, and holds her up as a pure and spotless friend and person.

Sally Hayes is a girl that Holden sometimes dates, though he thinks she is a "pain in the ass". She is sensible, practical, boring, and, in Holden's words, "phony as hell".

Ward Stradlater, Holden's roommate at Pencey Prep, is fairly conceited. He is a good-looking prep school athlete with a notorious history of having sex with girls. He has a date with Jane Gallagher in the beginning of the novel and fights with Holden when he returns from that date.

Robert Ackley is a boy who lives in the room next to Holden at Pencey Prep. He is, according to Holden, a "terrific bore" and a "slob" in personal hygiene. However, Holden is in his own way quite sympathetic toward Ackley and at times even seeks his company. Ackley seems even more pathetic than Holden, for his shabby physical appearance intensifies his isolation. Unlike Holden, Ackley wants to belong and constantly tries to gain acceptance, even from Holden. By contrast, Holden is self-alienated, purposely distancing himself from others and preferring his own thoughts to conversation.

Carl Luce is Holden's former academic advisor from Whooton and someone whom Holden considers to be both an intellectual and wise to the ways of the world.

Maurice is the sleazy elevator operator at the hotel in which Holden stays. In addition to this job, he is also a "pimp" and a bully.

Sunny is the young prostitute that Maurice sends to Holden's room. Though she seems very young, she is very businesslike and hardened.

Mrs. Morrow is the mother of a fellow student, Ernest Morrow, whom Holden dislikes intensely, though he praises him to Mrs. Morrow.

Holden meets **the two nuns** at a cafeteria in Grand Central. They have come from Chicago to teach in a school in New York. One of them is an English teacher and talks with Holden about *Romeo and Juliet*.

Mr. Spencer is Holden's history teacher from Pencey Prep. He shows a great deal of concern for Holden's future, but Holden thinks he is too old and pathetic.

Lillian Simmons is a woman D.B. used to date. A typical phony that Holden abhors, she loves to attract attention.

James Castle is a student at Elkton Hills who committed suicide.

Mal Brossard is Holden's friend at Pencey Prep.

Arthur Childs is a Quaker boy Holden knew at the Whooton School. Holden likes Arthur, but cannot "see eye to eye with him" because of his insistence that Holden read the Bible. Arthur Childs does not participate in the events of the novel; Holden merely mentions him.

Harris Macklin is a roommate of Holden's from the Elkton Hills school. Holden considers him boring, an incessant talker with a raspy voice. Harris does not participate in the events of the novel; Holden merely mentions him.

George something is a friend of Sally Hayes from Andover.

Rudolf Schmidt is the janitor in Holden's dorm.

Summary and Analysis

The Catcher in the Rye is a psychological novel based almost exclusively on how the unfolding events are interpreted by the protagonist, Holden Caulfield, and the consequences of those events on his emotional well-being. Episodic in nature, the novel is narrated in the form of flashbacks with an infinite number of digressions. These digressions provide a deeper understanding about the various characters and Holden's reaction to them. Most especially, however, these digressions tell us a great deal about Holden himself. The entire narrative of *The Catcher in the Rye* takes place during four days, and encompasses his decision to leave Pencey Prep before his formal expulsion, his decision to spend a few days in New York on his own before having to face his parents with the devastating news, and his odyssey in New York City before his eventual return home. Ultimately, his return home ends in his emotional breakdown and results in his being sent to a psychiatric facility for treatment.

Chapter 1 opens with Holden Caulfield speaking to a psychoanalyst about the circumstances surrounding his breakdown and immediately sets up his rebellious attitude towards the hypocrisy of society and those who manage its cultural and political institutions. Holden wastes no time in telling his therapist that he is not interested in discussing his childhood, but rather the events of the past four days that lead to his breakdown. "I'm not going to tell you my whole goddam autobiography or anything. I'll just tell you about this madman stuff that happened to me around last Christmas just before I got pretty run-down...." Having made this disclaimer, Holden launches into a recounting of his odyssey, replete with numerous digressions, which odyssey begins on a Saturday in December just before school closes for Christmas break. Indeed, the first digression takes place in the opening paragraph as we learn that his older brother, D.B., is a writer who abandoned a promising literary career to in order to pander to the tastes of Hollywood. "He's got a lot of dough now. He didn't *use* to. He used to be just a regular writer, when he was home." When Holden returns to his own story, he resumes his narrative by discussing the events surrounding his expulsion from Pencey Prep and his decision to spend a few days on his own in New York City before having to face his parents.

It is now Saturday afternoon, just a few days before Christmas vacation, and Holden is going to visit his history teacher, Mr. Spencer. With this final visit, Holden hopes to find some closure and, prior to reaching his destination, Holden gazes down from a hilltop overlooking Pencey, and recalls an early evening football game with two friends, a pleasant memory that will ease his conscience and make his leave-taking easier. Although he feels alienated from everyone and everything associated with the school, he nevertheless is desperately trying to feel some connection to the school before his precipitous departure. "I don't care if it's a sad good-by or a bad good-by, but when I leave a place I like to *know* I'm leaving it. If you don't, you feel even worse." However, these feelings notwithstanding, Holden is on his way to see his history teacher, old Mr. Spencer, in an attempt to make one final connection with someone at Pencey Prep.

Chapter 2 begins with a description of the Spencer household and quickly moves to Holden's very vivid account of his reaction towards Mr. Spencer's room. "The minute I went in, I was sort of sorry I'd come. He was reading the *Atlantic Monthly*, and there were pills and medicine all over the place, and everything smelled like Vicks Nose Drops. It was pretty depressing." Alas, although Holden was hoping to cement another positive memory with a member of the faculty, old Mr. Spencer is determined to turn the conversation into a discussion of Holden's failure in school and his pitiful career as a student. "He started handling my exam paper like it was a turd or something." Needless to say, while Spencer is determined to discuss Holden's shortcomings, Holden becomes increasingly impatient and irritated. Indeed, the visit becomes insufferable when Spencer forces Holden to listen as he reads aloud from Holden's wholly unsatisfactory essay on the mummies, "'[m]odern science would still like to know what the secret ingredients were that the Egyptians used when they wrapped up dead people so that their faces would not rot for innumerable centuries.'" Following this, old Spencer further exacerbates the situation by reading the note that Holden has written on the bottom of the report, apologizing for his failure to perform well on the paper. "[I]t is all right with me if you flunk me though as I am flunking everything else except English." Thus, the upshot of this visit with Spencer is that Holden is left once again with a desperate need to escape.

Chapter 3 begins with Holden giving us a few details about a former student of Pency Prep, the hypocritical Mr. Ossenburger, who became an undertaker. "He made a pot of dough in the undertaking business after he got out of Pencey.... He started these undertaking parlors all over the country that you could get members of your family buried for about five bucks." As a further morbid detail, Holden's dormitory is named after him—"the Ossenburger Memorial Wing." Following this bleak digression, Holden turns his attention to an important and recurring theme, namely his own reading habits, and lists his favorite authors: his brother D.B. (before he sold out to Hollywood), followed by Ring Lardner, Isak Dinesen, and Thomas Hardy. Indeed, Holden's ability to call upon the literary imagination is one of the most positive aspects of his character in that it allows him to transcend the hypocritical world he is forced to live in and allows a sympathetic communication with people he respects. "What really knocks me out is a book that, ... when you're all done reading it, you wish that the author that wrote it was a terrific friend of yours...." But, as he is settling down to read, a dorm neighbor, Robert Ackley, interrupts Holden, completely oblivious to Holden's rude hints that he is intruding. Holden's portrayal of Ackley is in fact revolting: "I never once saw him brush his teeth. They always looked mossy and awful, and he damn near made you sick if you saw him in the dining room with his mouth filled with mashed potatoes and peas or something." Nevertheless, Ackley is yet another alienated young man. Following this intrusion, Ward Stradlater,

Holden's athletic roommate, enters the room to get ready for a date and Ackley, who is always uncomfortable around Stradlater, quickly leaves.

Chapter 4 begins with Holden following Stradlater to the bathroom, where they spend some time talking. Stradlater asks Holden to write a descriptive essay for him, since he is going out on a date and will not have time. Holden reluctantly agrees, but becomes very anxious when he learns that Stradlater's date is none other than Jane Gallagher, a girl that Holden knows well from childhood and truly respects. Holden relates some thoughtful details about Jane's personality, with the anxiety that the sexy Stradlater will take advantage of her. For his part, Holden demonstrates his respect for Jane Gallagher when he remembers very particular details of the time he spent with her and took the time to learn who she truly was. While Holden affectionately describes her habits in playing checkers, "'she wouldn't move any of her kings.... She'd get them all lined up in the back row.... She just liked the way they looked. Stradlater is completely disinterested and quickly leaves as Holden sits in his room thinking about their date until Ackley returns. In **Chapter 5** Holden is at dinner in the dormitory, where steak is always served on Saturday night for the benefit of the parents visiting, yet another deliberately staged false impression about life a Pencey Prep. "What a racket. You should've seen the steaks. They were these little hard, dry jobs that you could hardly even cut." After dinner, Holden agrees to go to Agerstown with his friend Mel Brossard and Ackley, but since they have already seen the current movie, they eat hamburgers and play pinball before heading back to the dorm. Broussard goes to play cards, and Holden finally excuses himself to Ackley explaining that he has to write an essay – clearly the one Stradlater asked him to do. Holden's chosen theme is from the heart – a poignant description of the baseball glove that belonged to his deceased little brother Allie, who died from leukemia. Allie had written poems in green ink all over his baseball glove so he would have something to read when he played outfield. "The thing that was descriptive about it, though, was that he had poems written all over the fingers and the pocket and everywhere. In green ink. He wrote them so that he'd have something to read when he was in the field and nobody was up at bat." Holden cherishes this mitt and has kept it with him the whole time he was at school.

In **Chapter 6,** Stradlater returns in a terrible mood from his date with Jane Gallagher, complaining about how the dorm reminded him of a morgue with everyone gone. Furthermore, when Holden proudly gives him the descriptive essay he requested, Stradlater becomes angry with the portrayal of Allie's baseball mitt. In response to Stradlater's ingratitude, Holden takes the composition back from Stradlater and rips it up, for he too has been anxious the entire time that Stradlater was out with Jane. "He was unscrupulous. He really was." For his part, Stradlater responds cryptically as to how things turned out, "'[w]hat the hell ya think we did all night – play checkers, for Chrissake," which further infuriates Holden and precipitates a fight. Stradlater wins the fight easily, telling Holden to clean himself up, since he is a bloody mess. Holden goes in search of Ackley and, in **Chapter 7**, we find Holden asking Ackley if he can sleep in the vacant bed in Ackley's room. Ackley refuses with the ridiculous excuse that his roommate, Ely, who always goes home on weekends, might come back early and need his bed, all the while explaining that he. Ackley, needs to get up early for Mass the next day. Holden eventually leaves because Ackley refuses to acknowledge his need to talk to a friend. "I didn't want to hang around in that stupid room atmosphere any more." Feeling isolated and alone, Holden resolves to leave Pencey Prep immediately and go to New York, without telling anyone. Since it is too late to call a taxi, Holden decides to walk to the train station (**Chapter 8**). The train comes soon and is practically empty, although tonight Holden would actually prefer for it to be full. At Trenton station, a lady gets on and, when Holden recognizes Pencey Prep's insignia on one of her suitcases, he proceeds to engage her in conversation. It turns out that she is the mother of one of Holden's classmates, a boy named Ernest Morrow, another phony whom Holden holds in contempt. "Her son was doubtless the biggest bastard that ever when to Pencey, in the whole crumby history of the school." Nevertheless, his true feelings about Ernest notwithstanding, Holden spews a series of ingratiating lies about her son, the kind a mother wants to hear. "He's just got this very original personality that takes you a little while to get to know him." In the final scene with Mrs. Morrow, Holden displays his enormous creativity in fabricating an absurd identity when he tells her that his name is Rudolf Schmidt, the name of the janitor at the school and, furthermore, that he is on his way to have a tumor removed from his brain. "'Oh, I'll be all right and everything! It's right near the outside. And it's a very tiny one. They can take it out in about two minutes.'"

Upon his arrival at Penn Station in New York (**Chapter 9**), Holden considers calling someone, but emerges from the phone booth twenty minutes later having called no one. He walks to the taxi stand and hails one. Once he checks in at the sleazy Edmont Hotel, he gazes out of the window of his room, and is given an unexpected glimpse of some the "perverts and morons" across the way, including a cross-dresser. "I saw this one guy, a gray-haired, very distinguished looking guy with only his shorts on, do something you wouldn't believe me if I told you.... [H]e took out all these women's clothes and put them on. Then he started walking up and down the room, taking these very small steps, the way a woman does...." These garish sights cause Holden to thinks about calling Jane Gallagher but, instead, he calls a woman, ironically named Faith Cavendish, whom he does not know. Holden has gotten her telephone number from some "guy that went to Princeton," and, although she is not a prostitute, she supposedly "does not mind doing it once in a while." But even this superficial attempt to communicate with a stranger is doomed to failure. In fact, Faith sounds rather conventional, explaining that her roommate needs to get her sleep and pointing out that is the middle of the night and she needs to get her beauty rest. **Chapter 10** continues this desperate longing for communication with someone who understands him. Holden debates with himself as to whether he should call his beloved younger sister, Phoebe, but ultimately decides not to because his parents would be most likely to answer the phone. Having exhausted the list of people he would like to speak to but cannot, he is left with no alternative but to find some companionship in the Lavender Room, the nightclub at the Edmont Hotel. At the club, Holden is given a bad table, and the waiter refuses to serve him alcohol without an I. D. Three women are seated at the next table, and Holden summons up the courage to ask if any of them would care to dance. "I started giving the three witches at the next table they eye again.... I'm very fond of dancing, sometimes, and that was one of the times." He eventually dances with all three and pays for their drinks. When they get up to leave, he tries unsuccessfully to convince them to stay, even though they are not interesting company. Shortly after they depart, Holden leaves as well, returning to the lobby where he is once again consumed with his obsession concerning Jane and Stradlater's date and what really transpired. True to his far more sensitive consideration of others with whom he comes into contact, most especially women, Holden continues to reflect on the close relationship he once had with Jane. (**Chapter 11**). "I wouldn't exactly describe her as strictly beautiful. She knocked me out, though.... She was the only one, outside my family, that I ever showed Allie's baseball mitt to, with all the poems written on it." Holden also remembers a particularly touching moment when, while they were playing checkers, the mere presence of her stepfather has reduced her to tears, a reaction she tried to hide from him. "Then all of a sudden, this tear plopped down on the checkerboard.... She tried to rub it into the board with her fingers. I don't know why, but it bothered hell out of me." Thus, the checkerboard represents far more than a simple game. However, Holden's thoughts soon turn to his brother D.B. and he resolves to head for Ernie's bar in Greenwich Village that his brother used to take him to.

While riding in a taxi to Ernie's (**Chapter 12**), a very depressed Holden tries to strike up a conversation with the driver, Horowitz, and asks him if he knows where the Central Park ducks take refuge in winter. The insensitive taxi-driver is irritated by this question and shifts the conversation to a discussion of the fish in the pond which he believes have a much harder existence. Nevertheless, Holden is reluctant to dismiss yet another very unpromising chance for human companionship, and asks the taxi-driver to have a drink with him. Once again, Holden is rejected. Upon entering Ernie's, Holden is ushered to yet another bad table, where he is able to hear the disheartening conversations of the couples on either side of him. As Holden sits there smoking and drinking, a girl named Lillian Simmons comes up to him and asks about his brother D.B., whom she once dated. She introduces the sailor who is with her and asks Holden if he would like to join them. Holden refuses the offer, saying he is about to leave and is immediately upset that he told this lie, for he now feels compelled to leave rather than expose his false excuse. "I couldn't even stick around to hear old Ernie play something halfway decent.... People are always ruining things for me."

Chapter 13 opens with Holden walking back towards his hotel in the cold, lamenting the loss of his gloves, which he thinks were stolen by someone at Pencey. Hoping to warm up a little, Holden puts on his hunting hat and decides to stop in another bar, but is soon intimidated from so doing when he sees two tough looking guys emerging. Once back at the hotel, Holden is forced to confront the disreputable denizens of the hotel – in particular, a sleazy elevator operator named Maurice, who promises to send him a prostitute in fifteen minutes. Though Holden agrees to the solicitation, he immediately regrets having done so. "It was against my principles and all, but I was feeling so depressed.... When you're feeling very depressed, you can't even think." As he nervously awaits the arrival of the prostitute, the ironically named Sunny soon arrives, and Holden decides to conceal his identity once again, introducing himself as Jim Steele. As he further attempts to conceal his apprehension and the fact that he is a virgin, Holden's attempts at sophistication fail. By contrast, Sunny's demeanor is businesslike and only serves to accentuate Holden's feelings of awkwardness. When he tries to strike up a conversation, Sunny does not understand his delay and instead sits on his lap and tries to seduce him, thus forcing a very desperate Holden to end the charade. In his courtly way, he apologizes to Sunny, pays her the agreed upon sum of five dollars, and tells her to leave. However, when he refuses to pay her more than he agreed upon five dollars, she leaves with an insult.

(Chapter 14). After Sunny leaves, Holden smokes a few cigarettes and thinks about a time he refused to take his little brother Allie with him somewhere, a thought which depresses him greatly and he unexpectedly gets into bed with the urge to pray. "But while he tries to form the words of a prayer, he is stymied by the thoughts of Sunny calling him a "crumb-bum." While he is unable to calm down, there is an ominous knock on his door. Maurice and Sunny are waiting outside. Maurice demands another five dollars from Holden, insisting that the price was ten dollars. An outraged Holden refuses to pay in a voice that was "shaking like hell." As Maurice threatens him, "[c]hief, you're gonna force me inna roughin' ya up a little bit," Sunny enters Holden's room and takes an additional five dollars from his wallet. In response, Holden bursts into tears and challenges Maurice to a fight, a challenge which is met by Maurice punching Holden in the stomach. Holden falls to the floor, crying and hurt, as Maurice and Sunny leave. When he finally gets up, he collects his thoughts by imagining himself killing Maurice in the elevator. "I pictured myself coming out of the goddam bathroom, dressed and all, with my automatic in my pocket, and staggering around a little bit.... As soon as old Maurice opened the doors, he'd see me with the automatic in my hand, and he'd start screaming at me, in this very high-pitched, yellow-belly voice to leave him alone. But I'd plug him anyway." The chapter ends with Holden trying to calm himself by taking a bath and attempting to fall asleep. But he is depressed and tells us that he thought of committing suicide.

When he awakens around ten o'clock on Sunday morning (Chapter 15), he is about to call room service when the fear that Maurice will deliver the food takes hold and makes him change his mind. He also thinks about calling Jane Gallagher, but is not in the mood. Instead, he decides to call Sally Hayes, whom he has known for many years. "I used to think she was quite intelligent, in my stupidity. The reason I did was because she knew quite a lot about the theater and plays and literature and all that stuff." After making a date for two o'clock that afternoon, Holden realizes he does not have much money left. He determines to check out of the hotel, and instead takes a taxi to Grand Central Station where he can check his baggage into a locker and have breakfast in the cafeteria. While seated in the cafeteria, two nuns come and sit near him. Holden strikes up a conversation with them and, upon learning that one of them is an English teacher, the one with "the iron glasses," he proceeds to discuss literature with her. "Then I started wondering like a bastard what the one sitting next to me ... thought about, being a nun and all, when she read certain books.... Books not necessarily with a lot of sexy stuff in them, but books with lovers and all in them." However, they discuss Shakespeare's *Romeo and Juliet*, which Holden is a bit skittish about doing because "that play gets pretty sexy in some parts." Holden also notices their cheap suitcases, which make him think of Dick Slagle, whom he roomed with at Elkton Hills. Dick, like the nuns, had very cheap luggage, which he hid in shame under his bed. Holden, in contrast, had very nice, very expensive luggage that he at first kept on the racks for everyone to see but, in yet another demonstration of his sensitivity towards others, in this instance for his roommate Slagle, he tells us that he moved it under his bed. However, similar to the fate of Holden's many gestures of kindness and consideration, his graciousness towards Slagle is undermined, as the latter seizes the opportunity to replace Holden's luggage in the closet and pass it off as his own. The memory of this incident really bothers Holden, and he is not sure why; he thinks it has something to do with inequality and hypocrisy, two things he hates. The chapter concludes with Holden deciding to give the nuns a contribution of ten dollars despite the fact that he is low on funds. He even offers to pay their bill, but they refuse. After they leave, Holden wishes he had given them more than ten dollars.

Holden finishes his breakfast around noon and decides to take a walk since he has two hours to spare before his date with

Sally Hayes (**Chapter 16**). While he is walking, Holden cannot help but think about the nuns and their collection basket. This stirs his imagination about what his mother, aunt, and "Sally Hayes's crazy mother" would do if they were given the job of collecting money for charity. "My aunt's pretty charitable – she does a lot of Red Cross work and all – but she's very well-dressed and all, and when she does anything charitable she's always very well-dressed and has lipstick on and all that crap." Having no particular direction in mind, he finds himself walking toward Broadway and decides to stop by a record store and buy a record for Phoebe – a rare record called 'Little Shirley Beans' by "this colored girl singer, Estelle Fletcher." On his way, Holden comes across a poor family that he perceives has just come out of some church. The little boy, walking behind his parents, appears happy as he sings to himself and thus attracts Holden's attention. Indeed, the little boy's carefree attitude serves to alleviate some of Holden's depression. "He was singing that song, 'If a body catch a body coming through the rye.' ... It made me feel not so depressed any more."

Holden continues on his mission to buy Phoebe's favorite record and immediately finds it. Following this, he goes to a nearby drugstore to call Jane Gallagher, though he now has a date with Sally Hayes. This time he really does call her house, but hangs up when her mother answers. Holden then buys a newspaper, checks to see what is playing, and buys tickets for "I Know My Love." Though he has little interested in seeing play, he thinks Sally Hayes will love it. Holden then takes a taxi up to Central Park to look for Phoebe and give her the record, but she is not there. Holden starts walking toward the Museum of Natural History, reminiscing about past trips he has made there. "I knew that whole museum routine like a book....Sometimes we looked at the animals and sometimes we looked at the stuff the Indian had made in ancient times.... I loved that damn museum." When he arrives, he changes his mind about going in and instead heads for the Biltmore to meet Sally Hayes.

Holden arrives early for his date with Sally (**Chapter 17**), and indulges in some girl watching while he waits and launches into a digression on the boring guys that he imagines these girls are waiting for. "Guys that never read books. Guys that are very boring– ...." Finally, when Sally does arrive, ten minutes late, Holden excuses her because she looks so good. Holden has bought tickets for "the Lunts" – an American acting couple (Alfred Lunt and Lynn Fontanne) who appeared in the New York theatre scene, starring in sophisticated modern comedies and heavy dramas. Although we are not told specifically which play they see, Holden comments that "[i]t was about five hundred thousand years in the life of this one old couple....The trouble was, it was *too* much like people talking and interrupting each other." Nevertheless, he reluctantly admits the show is not bad. Afterward, Sally suggests they go ice skating at Radio City, mostly because she wants to rent one of those little skating skirts to show off her legs. However, both Holden and she are miserable skaters, and they finally retreat to the bar for cokes, where Holden is suddenly roused from his depression with the thought of running away. Though he asks Sally to go with him, she dismisses his idea as ridiculous and impractical. An argument ensues with Holden insulting her for not going along with his scheme to run away to the rural parts of Massachusetts or Vermont. "'You give me a royal pain in the ass, if you want to know the truth." Sally then leaves with hurt feelings and Holden concludes that he is "a madman.". With Sally gone, Holden realizes he is hungry and goes into a drugstore to buy a Swiss cheese sandwich and a malted milk **(Chapter 18)**. While in the drugstore, he decides to give Jane Gallagher another call, but she is not home. Running out of options, Holden finally decides to call Carl Luce, an older boy whom Holden knows from the Whooton School and whom he considers to be an intellectual. Although Holden does not particularly like Carl, he nevertheless arranges to meet him for a drink at ten o'clock at the Wicker Bar. To pass the time until ten o'clock, Holden goes to the movies at Radio City to pass the time, but enjoys neither the movie, about an English couple who love Charles Dickens and who "make a hatful of dough" by writing a book, nor the Christmas special presented beforehand.

Holden arrives at the Wicker Bar early and manages to find a seat (**Chapter 19**). The Wicker Bar, which is situated in the swanky Seton Hotel, often features Tina and Janine, who play the piano and sing silly songs in French and English. Although Holden recalls that this duo is not very talented, everyone else in the bar is enthusiastic, a fact which bothers him. "If you sat around there long enough and heard all the phonies applauding and all, you got to hate everybody in the world, I swear you did." While waiting for Carl, Holden drinks scotch and sodas and watches some gay guys at the bar, referring to them as "flits." He begins to think about sex, a subject that he expects he will have lots to talk about with Carl Luce. But, when Carl finally arrives and begins to drink, he appears uninterested and anxious to leave. At several points in the conversation, he tells Holden to grow up and quit being so childish. "I refuse to answer any typical Caulfield questions tonight. When in *hell* are you going to grow up?" As we have seen so many times before, Holden longs for some meaningful communication with another person and persists in talking to Carl though Carl does everything to dissuade him. Furthermore, Holden wants to discuss sex with Carl since it is an issue of overwhelming concern for him, but once again he can receive no guidance from someone whose opinion he respects. Instead, Holden is told to lower his volume. When Carl is ready to leave, Holden pleads with him to stay a little longer but, alas, Carl has had enough of him. As he departs he suggests that Holden be psychoanalyzed.

Holden remains at the Wicker Bar, getting drunk (**Chapter 20**). A singer named Valencia, accompanied by some "flitty looking guy with wavy hair," is performing. Holden prefers Valencia to Tina and Janine and asks the headwaiter to invite her to join him for a drink. Though it is unclear as to whether the waiter does not give her the message or she is not interested, Valencia exits quickly when her act is finished. In his drunken stupor, Holden begins once again to pretend he is wounded in the stomach as he keeps putting his hand under his jacket to prevent the bleeding, but shortly thereafter decides he would rather call Jane, but ends of phoning Sally

Hayes instead. Sally is not pleased with his phone call in the middle of the night and, realizing he is drunk, tells him to go home and go to bed and call her tomorrow. Before leaving the bar, Holden soaks his head in a basin full of cold water to sober up. Once outside, Holden starts walking toward Central Park to see for himself whether the ducks are safely taken care of, but has some difficulty finding the duck pond. When he finally reaches the lagoon, the ducks are gone, a fact which turns his thoughts once again to getting sick with pneumonia. "I started picturing millions of jerks coming to my funeral and all." He decides he wants to see Phoebe and makes his way towards home.

When Holden arrives at his apartment building (**Chapter 21**), he believes that he had a lucky break because the elevator operator is a substitute who does not recognize him, thus enabling him to remain unknown to all but his sister Phoebe. Holden makes up a silly lie, that he is here to see the Dicksteins, which ends up confusing the elevator boy enough that he lets Holden up without asking too many questions. Since he has the house key, he makes his way on tiptoe through the apartment to Phoebe's room. When she is not in her bed, Holden remembers that she sometimes sleeps in D.B.'s room. "You ought to see her doing her homework or something at that crazy desk.... She says she likes to spread out. That kills me. What's old Phoebe got to spread out.?" He finds her sleeping soundly and watches for awhile. Before he wakes her, Holden sits down at the desk and reads one of her school notebooks. As expected, Phoebe is thrilled to see him. She tells him about all the recent happenings in her life while Holden listens lovingly to her. After telling Holden that their parents are at a party in Connecticut and will not be home until late, she quickly realizes that he is home from Pencey earlier than he should be and asks if he has been kicked out again. Though Holden tries to lie his way out of the situation, Phoebe sees through him and gets upset, so much so that she covers her head with a pillow and refuses to talk to him. Though Holden tries to coax Phoebe out of her anger, she remains bitterly disappointed knowing that the family will once again be thrown into chaos with the news of Holden's most recent expulsion (**Chapter 22**). Each time Holden tries to steer the conversation away from his actions, Phoebe draws him back in, challenging him to name any one thing that he really likes, and asks him what he would like to become. After some thought Holden tells her that he wants to be a catcher in the rye. "'Anyway, I keep picturing all these little kids playing some game in this big field of rye and all.... And I'm standing on the edge of some crazy cliff.... I'd have to come out from somewhere and *catch* them. That's all I'd do all day.'" However, Phoebe's response after a long silence is, "Daddy's going to kill you." Holden responds by saying that he does not care and then resolves to call Mr. Antolini, his English teacher from Elkton Hills.

Holden's phone conversation with Mr. Antolini is, by necessity, abbreviated, for he is afraid his parents may return any moment and find him at home (**Chapter 23**). Mr. Antolini graciously invites Holden to come over even though it is late at night. It is interesting to note that given the disastrous events of his prior visit with Mr. Spencer, the prognosis for his imminent meeting with Antolini might very well be an ominous one, though Holden is not conscious of this. Nevertheless, despite his urgency to leave home quickly, Holden is reluctant to leave his affectionate reunion with Phoebe. When he returns to his room to gather his things, Phoebe has turned on the radio and Holden takes time out to dance four different numbers with her. After a while, while they are resting, Phoebe hears their parents come in and hurriedly switches off the light. Holden puts out his cigarette and hides in the closet. When their mother comes into the room to check on her, she smells smoke. For her part, Phoebe protects her brother by placing the blame on herself and says that she is the one who has been smoking. When their mother finally leaves, Holden comes out of the closet and asks her to loan him some money. As she willingly hands over all her Christmas dough, Holden quite unexpectedly begins to cry. His tears flow for a long time before he sneaks out of the house. However, once outside, Holden almost wishes his parents had caught him, though it remains only a wish.

Holden is now on his way to Mr. and Mrs. Antolini, who live on Sutton Place, one of the most expensive streets in Manhattan (**Chapter 24**). While on his way in a cab to the Antolinis, Holden complains of being dizzy and will remains so once he arrives at the Antolini household. Once there, Holden learns that Antolini has been genuinely concerned about him, so much so that he has recently met with Mr. Caulfield to discuss Holden's problems. On the subject of digressions, which Holden cannot help but give in to while telling us his story, their conversation becomes almost philosophical. "'Don't you think there's a time and place for everything? Don't you think that if someone starts out to tell you about his father's farm, he should stick to his guns, *then* get around to tell you about his uncle's brace.'"? And Holden's response is to defend digressions on the grounds that you never know in advance how your narrative will play out. "'What I think is, you're supposed to leave somebody alone if he's at least being interesting and he's getting all excited about something.'" Holden is angry when someone tries to stifle his imagination. Antolini then warns Holden about people who destroy themselves by "looking for something their own environment couldn't supply them with" and admonishes him that he must overcome this problem. Education, he further explains, will help Holden realize that he is not alone in his alienation from the world around him and far from "the first person who was ever confused and frightened and even sickened by human behavior." However, though Antolini's advice might very will alleviate Holden's bleak perspective, Antolini spoils the support and nurturing he has given his former student, by putting his hand on Holden's forehead, which the latter interprets as a possible sexual advance. Holden leaves precipitously, stating that he must get back to Grand Central Station to claim his bags.

Following this latest trauma, Holden next wakes up from a nap in Grand Central Station, and starts to wonder if he has perhaps misinterpreted Antolini's gesture as the act of a pervert (**Chapter 25**). "I mean I wondered if just maybe I was wrong about thinking he was making a flitty pass at me.... I mean how can you tell about that stuff for sure." However, despite his doubts about Antolini's intentions, Holden remains alone and ill, his physical symptoms from the night before having only intensified. While wandering the streets of Manhattan on this Monday morning, Holden sees the dual aspects of beauty and ugliness in the landscape, from the use of profanity by a man who is unloading a Christmas tree from a truck to the beauty of Fifth Avenue, filled with shoppers during the holidays. Feeling somewhat cheerful now as he remembers the fun he has had with Phoebe, Holden walks toward Central Park. However, this happiness is fleeting as Holden returns to his habitual dreariness and becomes anxious that he is about to disappear, a dreariness which causes him to call upon Allie for help. "I thought I'd just go down, down, down, and nobody'd ever see me again." Finally, after walking a couple of miles, Holden sits down on a park bench, perspiring and breathing heavily, at which time he fabricates a plan to escape this troubled world for good. Holden dreams of cutting himself off from all humanity by pretending to be a deaf mute. "If anybody wanted to tell me something, they'd have to write it on a piece of paper and shove it over to me....Everybody'd think I was just a poor deaf-mute bastard and they'd leave me alone." Having resolved to do this, Holden decides to stop by Phoebe's school in order to have a goodbye note delivered to her in class. On his way to the principal's office, Holden once again sees ugliness in the form of obscenities scrawled on the wall, which nearly devastates him. So disturbed is he when he considers how small children are going to see this obscenity, that he rubs the words out with his hand, intent on keeping the children from being hurt by this vileness.

Holden next heads for the Metropolitan Museum of Art where he will wait for Phoebe. While there, he talks with two children who are playing hooky from school and have come to see the Egyptian mummies and he is quite enthusiastic when he tells them how interesting the exhibit is. Once the boys leave, Holden enjoys the peace and quiet in the tomb, only to be rudely interrupted by another obscenity scrawled on the wall.

However, this time he makes a joke about the obscenity, albeit a bitter one, a sign that Holden may be starting to take the world a little differently. Interestingly, Holden now expands on his daydream of running away, by including a trip back home when he's about thirty-five, and receiving occasional visits from Phoebe and D.B. He seems now to be less determined to cut himself off completely. Finally, this connectedness comes back to him in a second and more realistic way when Phoebe shows up with a suitcase so that she can run away with her brother, firmly refusing to listen to any plan of his that doesn't include her. Ultimately, she tells Holden to shut up, for the very first time and, as Holden tells us, "[i]t sounded terrible. God, it sounded terrible. It sounded worse than swearing." Holden also now recognizes that the innocence of childhood is fragile and fleeting and that Phoebe's wish to go with him is part of a continuing cycle of growth and change. Phoebe and Holden then make their way to the zoo, though they are not speaking to or walking with each other, and eventually arrive at the carrousel and Holden buys a ticket for his sister. As he watches her riding around and around, Holden understands that he must let go of his wish to see her as an eternal child. "The thing with kids is, if they want to grab for the gold ring, you have to let them do it, and not say anything. If they fall off, they fall off, but it's bad if you say anything to them" Chapter 25 ends with Holden having achieved a newfound happiness.

Chapter 26 finds Holden speaking to the analyst at some undisclosed mental health facility, saying that he cannot say much more because it is irrelevant. Holden somewhat regrets having discussed his private experiences with so many people, because in a way he misses the people he has spoken of. Hence, he concludes with this advice to his readers – "Don't ever tell anybody anything. If you do, you start missing everybody."

Critical Views

CARL F. STRAUCH ON THE COMPLEXITY OF HOLDEN'S CHARACTER

If Holden's suffering is the measure as well as the product, in part, of the outrageous assault on private innocence by social depravity, it does not follow that Salinger's philosophy is Rousseauistic. If we acknowledge that a personality has been split to the very core, such a discovery does not support the view that Holden, unlike the resourceful Huck, wishes to remain immature. Nor, as we shall learn, does the conclusion of *The Catcher* present a "creed" of any kind in the sense demanded by one critic; and the conclusion, furthermore, is neither pessimistic nor, for that matter, ironical in any sense perceived thus far. An immature Holden is not being delivered up to the unmerciful process of adjustment to a society he detests. The irony is profounder than that because the meaning is profounder: a Holden who has accepted both the mood and the act of responsibility with Phoebe does not require psychoanalytic therapy, for he has miraculously wrought his own cure and has thus spiritually escaped the social rigidities that would be imposed upon him. The conclusion is, therefore, optimistic and affirmative, not in any credal sense but in terms of the unconquerable resources of personality.

Now, the thesis of the present study is that all or most of this psychological and philosophical insight can be gained only through a recognition of the interlocking metaphorical structure of *The Catcher*. We may thus perceive that Salinger has employed neurotic deterioration, symbolical death, spiritual awakening, and psychological self-cure as the inspiration and burden of an elaborate pattern—verbal, thematic, and episodic, that yields the meaning as a discursive examination of Holden's character and problem out of metaphoric context can never do. Structure is meaning.

As a start, the readiest way of understanding *The Catcher* lies in an awareness of the dualism or ambivalence of language, for Holden employs both the slob and the literate idiom. He mingles them so nicely, however, and with such colloquial ease that the alternating modes have heretofore escaped attention; and however we look at the two languages, each is, in effect, employed both realistically and metaphorically. Holden's slob language is obviously justified as a realistic narrative device, since it is the idiom of the American male; yet from the psychological point of view, it becomes the boy's self-protective, verbalized acceptance of the slob values of his prep school contemporaries. He thus may justify himself in his overt being and may hope to secure immunity from attack and rationalize his "belonging"; slob language, therefore, hits off two important social themes—security and status. But the psychological intent becomes symbolical portent when we see that the mass idiom emphasizes a significant distinction between two worlds—the phony world of corrupt materialism and Holden's private world of innocence which, in its corporate love, embraces a secret goldfish, Holden's dead brother Allie, his sister Phoebe (all children, in fact), Jane Gallagher, nuns, and animals (ducks and zoo animals, the Doberman that belonged to Jane's family, and the dog that Olivier- Hamlet patted on the head). For his private world Holden uses a literate and expressive English, and so the profounder psychological and symbolical purposes of slob language may be detected only as that idiom functions in polarized relationship with the other. We need not labor the point that the full range of Salinger's portrayal would never be disclosed without an awareness of the ambivalence of language.

The literary Salinger has, of course, created a literate and even literary and artistic Holden, capable of acute aesthetic as well as moral judgments. Thus, Ernie, the piano player in Greenwich Village, was phony in his mingled real snobbery and false humility, and the Lunts overdid their acting and were *too* good. It is such a perceptive Holden that opens the narrative on a confessional note—"all that David Copperfield kind of crap"; and it may be observed in passing, as a literary parallel, that if Dickens portrays a young Victorian immoralist, Steerforth, Salinger gives us Stradlater, a "secret slob" and "sexy bastard." Holden's literary taste provides depth of background for a boy who said of himself, "I'm quite illiterate, but I read a lot." Favorite authors are his own brother D.B., Ring Lardner, and Thomas Hardy. Holden dismisses Hemingway as phony but approves of Fitzgerald's *The Great Gatsby*, from which, amusingly, he has borrowed Gatsby's nonchalant and phony habit of address—"old sport"; thus, Holden refers to "old Spender," "old Mrs. Morrow," "old Ernie," "old Phoebe." If this literary borrowing represents merely Holden's linguistic "horsing around," there is, on the other hand, real bite to his reporting Allie's verdict that Emily Dickinson was a better war poet than Rupert Brook, the idea being that imagination imparts meaning to experience; and the discerning reader will keep this in mind as a gloss for Holden's concluding observation on his traumatic adventures.

Presumably, Holden's literary judgments are as perceptive as Allie's. Holden "wouldn't mind calling ... up" Isak Dinesen, the author of *Out of Africa*; and his reason, open to readers of the Danish noblewoman, spring from his own suffering, for a writer so warmly understanding of children and animals would make an appropriate *confidante*. The slob Holden is more prominent, but the literate Holden is more intrinsic, for like Isak Dinesn he can use language to express sensitive insights and human joys. As we proceed we shall note that although some of the literary sophistication is solely for background, a few works enter into and reinforce the moral, psychological, and symbolic range of *The Catcher*.

The literary precision with which Holden employs slob language for a public world that is varyingly indifferent and cruel and usually phony and literate speech for his private world emerges beautifully when he explains how he met Jane Gallagher: "The way I met her, this Doberman pinscher she had used to come over and *relieve* himself on our lawn, and my mother got very irritated about it. My mother can make a very big stink about that kind of stuff" (italics mine).

Once we have recognized the ambivalence of language we are prepared to discover Salinger's elaborate use of several kinds of pattern that support and help to develop the narrative.

The first verbal pattern to be examined stands in an ironic and mutually illuminating relationship with the image of the secret goldfish at the head of the narrative symbolizing Holden and his secret world. In D.B.'s short story "The Secret Goldfish" the boy would not let others see the goldfish "because he'd bought it with his own money." Holden likewise was to pay in far more than money for his secret world; and as a further parallel, nobody ever saw (or cared to see) this secret world, although Holden invites inspection in the confessional mode, "if you really want to hear about it." This mode is maintained throughout with frequent interpolations of "if you want to know the truth" or "if you really want to know." As the story uncovers more and more of Holden's dilemma, these phrasings, although employed in the most casual manner, transcend their merely conversational usage and become psychologically portentous. The inference is that society, including his own parents, has no desire to recognize the truth about Holden or its own obsessions. In the middle of the tale Holden learns from the psychoanalytic snob, Carl Luce, that his father had helped him to "adjust"; and the blunted resolution of the narrative on the Freudian couch represents society's final humiliating indifference to truth. Recognition of the truth would embrace the love and compassion that it has not time for but that Holden himself not only lavishes on his secret world but extends to the public world in episodes and reflections rounded off with a minor verbal pattern, "You felt sort of sorry for her" or "I felt sorry as hell for him."

(...)

In its emphasis on the conflict between the organic and the mechanistic, the secret and the public, reality and appearance, awakening and death, *The Catcher* hits off the strongest Romantic affirmations from Goethe and Wordsworth down to Lawrence, Joyce, and Hesse. Whether at Walden Pond, at Weissnichtwo, or in New York hot spots, the problem of personality remains; one surmises that, after a century and more, as *A Portrait of the Artist* and *Steppenwolf* likewise indicate, the struggle has become intensified. At the close of *The Catcher* the gap between society and the individual has widened perceptibly; and far from repudiating Holden's secret world, Salinger has added a secret of psychological depth. A mechanistic society, represented just as much by Antolini as by the psychoanalyst, may with the glib teacher continue to ignore the boy and talk of "what kind of thoughts your particular size mind should be wearing"; we may all comfort ourselves with the reflection that, after all, Holden is another bothersome case of arrested development, albeit rather charming in a pathetic and oafish manner.

ROBERT M. SLABEY ON CHRISTIAN THEMES AND SYMBOLS

The triduum of *The Catcher in the Rye* is made up of Saturday, Sunday, and Monday, December 17, 18, and 19, 1949. According to Christian observance the first two days would be Ember Saturday and the Fourth Sunday of Advent respectively. Advent is most closely kept by the more liturgical of the Christian sects. References are made to one of these, Catholicism. Several boys in the schools Holden attended are Catholics. Holden, whose father is an ex-Catholic, feels that Catholics in general tend to form cliques. (One son in Salinger's prodigious Glass family is a Catholic priest and like Salinger's parents, Mrs. Glass is Christian, Mr. Glass, Jewish.) Holden is not a churchgoer, hates ministers, and says that "all the children in [his] family are atheists" (p. 92),[1] but he admires the Biblical Jesus and in many respects thinks of himself as a messianic figure. he is disgusted by the phony and hypocritical Christianity of people like the philanthropist-undertaker Ossenburger (pp. 18-19).

The traditional purpose of Advent is to prepare for the coming of Christ—to recall His birth, to anticipate His second coming at the end of time, and to invite Him into the hearts of the faithful. I feel that all three aspects of Advent function in the symbolic patters of *The Catcher in the Rye*. The journey of the Holy Family is read during the season, with Mary one of the prominent figures in the orations and in the popular mind. Holden's memorable account of his breakfast with the traveling nuns in Grand Central Station establishes a connection with this feature. Holden admires the nuns' maternal qualities as well as their virginal innocence. (It is common knowledge that nearly all Catholic nuns bear some form of the name Mary.) Holden feels that the "Nativity" show at Radio City Music Hall presents the Christmas story (the Incarnation of Love) in a sentimental and phony manner.

> It's suppose to be religious as hell, I know, and very pretty and all, but I can't see anything religious or pretty, for God's sake, about a bunch of actors carrying crucifixes all over the stage. When they were all finished and started going out the boxes again, you could tell they could hardly wait to get a cigarette or something. I saw it with old Sally Hayes the year before, and she kept saying how beautiful it was, the costumes and all. I said old Jesus probably would've puked if He could see it ... (p. 125)[2]

Advent commemorates the time between the Fall and the Redemption. The physical atmosphere of *The Catcher in the Rye* reflects this in its cold and darkness. And the implication is that the estrangement and isolation of man are not only physical, moral, and psychological, but metaphysical and theological as well. it is a world in which the absence of God is felt. And Original Sin is one of the major themes of the novel. The semipenitential character of the Advent season, indicated by the use of purple vestments at Mass, reminds man that penance and contrition are necessary. The lesson of humility is one which Holden has to learn; in this respect, even the décor of the nightclub in his hotel is fitting: it is the Lavender Room. There are in the Advent liturgy reminders of the radical change effected in man's life by the Word Made Flesh: men are given power of becoming real children of god. Advent is a reminder that although Christ has come, the transformation of individual human lives is yet to be accomplished. One of Holden's recurrent activities is waking people up—his dormitory mates at Pencey, Sally Hayes, Phoebe, the Antolinis, Sunny, and Faith Cavendish; but Holden himself is not fully awake to himself and to the world.

The principal setting of the novel, New York City, is the spiritual wasteland of Isaiah; it is associated with Biblical places which in the prophetic literature are traditional images of the bondage of man before the Incarnation: Babylon, Sodom-Gomorrha, and Egypt. The Babylon-New York association is not new. New York has often been described as the city of wealth and dissipation as well as the city of the Anti-Christ. (The Babylonian captivity of the Jews was broken by Cyrus, a savior of his people and a prefiguration of the Messiah.) The prostitute Sunny's profession is appropriate to Babylon, while her pastime (move-going) is appropriate to New York. Because of the prevalence of perverts New York becomes another Sodom and Gomorrha. Holden's strong olfactory sense makes him keenly aware of the city's decadence, fetulence, and sickness. He sometimes outdoes his former classmate Carl Luce, "sexpert" and son of a psychiatrist, in identifying perverts; and he is repulsed by any hint of homosexuality. The bondage of the Israelites in Egypt and the promise of a Redeemer figure in the prophecies of Isaiah read during Advent. Holden's history paper concerns Egypt and he visits the Egyptian exhibit in the Metropolitan Museum. The Biblical significance of Egypt is asserted in a passage in Holden's examination found in Salinger's *Collier's* version but not in the novel: "... you read about them [the Egyptians] frequently in the Bible. The Bible is full of amusing anecdotes about the old Pharoahs ..."[3] Manhattan is an island, its inhabitants "*Isolatoe*s," as Ishmael called the crew of the *Pequod*, men "not acknowledging the common continent of men, but each *Isolato* living on a separate continent of his own." Holden is aware of his isolation; and he is constantly seeking love and communion.

Notes

1. All page references are to the Signet edition of *The Catcher in the Rye* (New York, 1961).

2. The play which Holden attends, *I Know My Love*, and the *Random-Harvest*-like movie are both romantic dramas which picture love enduring through the years. The movie is the major anachronism in the book. S. N. Behrman's play was on Broadway in December 1949, but the film at Radio City was the musical *On the Town*; *Random Harvest* played the Music Hall during the Christmas season of 1942. In a preliminary version of Holden's date with Sally ("Slight Rebellion Off Madison" [New Yorker, Dec. 21, 1946]) the play was Terence Rattigan's *O Mistress Mine*, the Lunts vehicle that year.

3. "I'm Crazy," *Collier's*, CXVI (Dec. 22, 1945), 48.

JONATHAN BAUMBACH ON SPIRITUALITY

J. D. Salinger's first and only novel, *The Catcher in the Rye* (1951), has undergone in recent years a steady if over insistent devaluation. The more it becomes academically respectable, the more it becomes fair game for those critics who are self-sworn to expose every manifestation of what seems to them a chronic disparity between appearance and reality. It is critical child's play to find fault with Salinger's novel. Anyone can see that the prose is mannered (the pejorative word for stylized); no one actually talks like its first-person hero Holden Caulfield. More over, we are told that Holden, as poor little rich boy, is too precocious and specialized an adolescent for his plight to have larger-than-prep-school significance. The novel is sentimental; it loads the deck for Holden and against the adult world; the small but corrupt group that Holden encounters is not representative enough to permit Salinger his inclusive judgments about the species. Holden's relationship to his family is not explored: we meet his sister Phoebe, who is a younger version of himself, but his father never appears, and his mother exits in the novel only as another voice from a dark room. Finally, what is Holden (or Salinger) protesting against but the ineluctability of growing up, of having to assume the prerogatives and responsibilities of manhood? Despite these objections to the novel, *Catcher in the Rye* will endure both because it has life and because it is a significantly original work, full of insights into at least the particular truth of Holden's existence. Within the limited terms of its vision, Salinger's small book is an extraordinary achievement; it is, if such a distinction is meaningful, an important minor novel.

Like all of Salinger's fiction, *Catcher in the Rye* is not only about innocence, it is actively for innocence—as if retaining one's childness were an existential possibility. The metaphor of the title-Holden's fantasy-vision of standing in front of a cliff and protecting playing children from falling (Falling)—is, despite the impossibility of its realization, the only positive action affirmed in the novel. It is, in Salinger's Manichean universe of child angels and adult "phonics," the only moral alternative—otherwise all is corruption. Since it is spiritually as well as physically impossible to prevent the Fall. Salinger's idealistic heroes are doomed either to suicide (Seymour) or insanity (Holden, Sergeant X) or mysticism (Franny), the ways of sainthood, or to moral dissolution (Eloise D. B., Mr. Antolini), the way of the world. In Salinger's finely honed prose, at once idiomatically real and poetically stylized, we get the terms of Holden's ideal adult occupation:

> Anyway, I keep picturing all these little kids playing some game in this big field of rye and all. Thousands of little kids, and nobody's around—nobody big, I mean— except me. And I'm standing on the edge of some crazy cliff. What I have to do, I have to catch everybody if they start to go over the cliff—I mean if they're running and they don't look where they're going I have to come out from somewhere and *catch* them. That's all I'd do all day. I'd just be the catcher in the rye and all. I know it's crazy, but that's the only thing I'd really like to be. I know it's crazy. [1]

Apparently Holden's wish is purely selfless. What he wants, in effect, is to be a saint—the protector and savior of innocence. But what he also wants, for he is still one of the running children himself, is that someone prevent *his* fall. This is his paradox: he must leave innocence to protect innocence. At sixteen, he is ready to shed his innocence and move like Adam into the fallen adult world, but he resists because those no longer innocent seem to him foolish as well as corrupt. In a sense, then, he is looking for an exemplar, a wise-good father whose example will justify his own initiation into manhood. Before Holden can become a catcher in the rye, he must find another catcher in the rye to show him how it is done.

Immediately after Holden announces his "crazy" ambition to Phoebe, he calls up one of his former teachers, Mr. Antolini, who is both intelligent and kind—a potential catcher in the rye.

> He was the one that finally picked up that boy that jumped out of the window I told you about, James Castle. Old Mr. Antolini felt his poise and all, and then he took off his coat and put it over James Castle and carried him all the way over to the infirmary. (p. 226).

Though Mr. Antolini is sympathetic because "he didn't even give a damn if his coat got all bloody," the incident is symbolic of the teacher's failure as a catcher in the rye. For all his good intentions, he was unable to catch James Castle or prevent his fall; he could only pick him up after he had died. The episode of the suicide is one of the looming shadows darkening Holden's world; Holden seeks out Antolini because he hopes that the gentle teacher—the substitute father—will "pick him up" before he is irrevocably fallen. Holden's real guest throughout the novel is for a spiritual father (an innocent adult). He calls Antolini after all the other fathers of his would have failed him, including his real father, whose existence in the novel is represented solely by Phoebe's childish reiteration of "Daddy's going to kill you." The fathers in Salinger's child's-eye world do not catch falling boys—who have been thrown out of prep school—but "kill" them. Antolini represents Holden's last chance to find a catcher-father. But his inability to save Holden has been prophesied in his failure to save James Castle; the episode of Castle's death provides an anticipatory parallel to Antoilini's unwitting destruction of Holden.

That Antolini's kindness to Holden is motivated in part by a homosexual interest, though it comes as a shock to Holden, does not wholly surprise the reader. Many of the biographical details that Salinger has revealed about him through Holden imply this possibility. For example, that he has an older and unattractive wife whom he makes a great show of kissing in public is highly suggestive; yet the discovery itself—Holden wakes to find Antolini sitting beside him and caressing his head—has considerable impact. We experience a kind of shock of recognition, the more intense for its having been anticipated. The scene has added power because Antolini is, for the most part, a good man, whose interest in Holden is genuine as well as perverted. His advice to Holden is apparently well-intentioned. Though many of his recommendations are cleverly articulated platitudes. Antolini evinces a prophetic insight when he tells Holden, "I have a feeling that you're riding for some kind of a terrible, terrible fall"; one suspects, however, that to some extent he is talking about himself. Ironically, Antolini becomes the agent of his "terrible, terrible fall" by violating Holden's image of him, by becoming a false father. having lost his respect for Antolini as a man, Holden rejects him as an authority; as far as Holden is concerned, Antolini's example denies the import of his words. His disillusionment with Antolini, who had seemed to be the sought-for, wise-good father, comes as the most intense of a long line of disenchantments; it is the final straw that breaks Holden. It is the equivalent of the loss of God. The world, devoid of good fathers (authorities), becomes a soul-destroying chaos in which his survival is possible only through withdrawal into childhood, into fantasy, into psychosis.

The action of the novel is compressed into two days in which Holden discovers through a series of disillusioning experiences that the adult world is unreclaimably corrupt. At the start of the novel, we learn from Holden that he has flunked out of Pencey Prep for not applying himself; he has resisted what he considers foolish or "phony" authority. Like almost all of Salinger's protagonists, Holden is clearly superior to his surroundings; he functions by dint of his pure sight, his innocence and sensibility, as initiate in and conscience of the world of the novel. Allowing for the exaggerations of innocence, we can generally accept Holden's value judgments of people and places as the judgments of the novel.

Note
1. J. D. Salinger, The Catcher in the Rye (Boston 1951), pp. 224–25; all pages references are to this edition.

JOHN M. HOWELL ON T.S. ELIOT'S INFLUENCE

"Not wasteland, but a great inverted forest with all foliage underground."
—Raymond Ford, "The Inverted Forest" (1947)

"Ah, Sharon Lipschutz,...How that name comes up. Mixing memory and desire....Sybil, I'll tell you what we'll do. We'll see if we can catch a bananafish."
—Seymour Glass, "A Perfect Day for Bananafish" (1948)

"He wrote this terrific book of short stores, *The Secret Goldfish*...Now he's out in Hollywood, D. B., being a prostitute."
—Holden Caulfield, *The Catcher in the Rye* (1951)

This brief dialogue is the essence of my argument that J. D. Salinger, "a dash man and not a miler," [1] found in T. S. Eliot's *The Waste Land* a controlling metaphor for his only published novel to date, *The Catcher in the Rye*.

I. THEME

In 1946, Salinger had a ninety-page version of *The Catcher* accepted for publication—but then withdrew it for revision and expansion. [2] One year later he published "The Inverted Forest," the first story to make obvious use of the waste land motif. Raymond Ford, the protagonist, is, like Holden's brother, D. B., a successful writer—a poet who lives in an emotional limbo which he characterizes as "Not wasteland but an inverted forest / with all foliage underground." [3] As he says, "The place where Alph, the sacred river, ran—was found out not invented" (p. 124). To find the underground forest he must "ford" the sacred river. This he cannot do. Ultimately, he deserts his wife, Corinne, whose resultant fantasy prefigures Holden's dream of being a "catcher in the rye"[4]:...a gallant file of people was approaching the precipice of her brain. One by one—she couldn't stop them—they dived off" (p. 129).

Tom Davis points out that Holden's idealized role as "catcher" strongly resembles that of the bodhisattva in Mahayana Buddhism who devoted himself to helping mankind find release from the wheel of birth and death. He quotes a passage from the Vajradhvaja *Sutra*, which concludes, "I must rescue all these being from the stream of Samsara...I must pull them back from the great precipice." [5] Davis says that Samsara is the process of reincarnation, and that the carrousel that Phoebe rides at the end of the novel is probably an allusion to the Buddhist Wheel. He might also have mentioned, as Jessie L. Weston does in *From Ritual to Romance*, that in Mahayana scriptures the "Buddha is referred to as the Fisherman who draws fish from the ocean of Samsara to the light of Salvation."[6] Miss Weston was concerned, as I am, with the Fisher King; and it was from her, along with H. C. Warren's *Buddhism in Translation* and Sir James G. Frazer's *The Golden Bough*, that Eliot got his central motifs: Grail and Tarot cards, Fisher King and Grail Knight, waste land and regenerative water, Buddhist Wheel and Fire Sermon.

(...)

D. B.'s story is "about a little kid that wouldn't let anybody look at his goldfish because he'd bought it with his own money" (p. 5). At one point Holden says, "If we had any children, we'd hide them somewhere" (p. 179). But the significance of the "fish" is most clearly dramatized by Holden's repeated questions about the frozen lagoon in Central Park, which functions, like Eliot's Thames in winter, as a pervasive symbol of sterility. In probably the single most amusing sequence in the novel, a taxi driver named Horwitz, in response to Holden's obsessive question about where the ducks go in the winter, answers instead, just as compulsively about the fish: "They get frozen right in one position for the whole winter...If you was a fish, Mother natur'd take care of *you*, wouldn't she? Right? You don't think them fish just die when it gets to be winter, do ya?" (pp. 76-77).

Holden's fantasy world is similarly frozen, and he finds his metaphor in the glass cases of the Indian Room at the Museum of Natural History. Here, in a huge aquarium where no fish swims, time is arrested as Holden would have it; a world where birds are always "flying south for the winter," where an Eskimo is always "fishing over a hole in this icy lake,..." (p. 110). In a key thematic statement, Holden says "Certain things they should stay the way they are. You ought to be able to stick them in one of those glass cases and just leave them alone" (p. 111). This is, of course, the "immortality" that he would like to give Phoebe—the existence of the Sybil who begs for death in *The Waste Land*'s epigraph. A few years later, in "De Daumier-Smith's Blue Period," Salinger's protagonist looks into a glass case of medical supplies and says "I would always at best be a visitor in a garden of enamel urinals and bedpans, with a sightless wooden dummy-deity standing by in a marked-down rupture truss."[8] Holden is at best a visitor in a world of perpetual "winter," where a fisherman is always fishing, but catching no fish, and Allie is dead, and the people are spiritually sterile.

Although Holden does not recognize the sterility of his idealized world, he does see the sterility of D. B.'s: "The goddam movies. they can ruin you" (p. 96). they have ruined D. B., his brother, and they are now threatening Phoebe, who excitedly tells Holden about *The Doctor*, another obvious analogue to Holden's "catcher" fantasy: "It was all about this doctor ... that sticks a blanket over this child's face that's a cripple and can't walk ... He was a mercy Killer. Only, he knows he deserves to go to jail because a doctor isn't supposed to take things away from God" (p. 47). Implication almost becomes statement, a moment later, when Phoebe, learning that Holden has been kicked out of Pencey, flops on her bed and puts a "pillow over her head" (p. 149). "The Catcher," the "Eskimo," and the "Doctor" are at one with the "Sybil": the fish, once caught is dressed in a shroud.

What is the proper way to "catch" fish? Allie, Holden's dead brother, has said that Emily Dickinson is a better war poet that Rupert Brooke (p. 127), and has left behind a baseball mitt covered with her poems (just as Seymour leaves a bedroom door covered with inspirational quotations[9]). Allie's glove is, then, a kind of spiritual gauntlet which Holden as "catcher" must carry into the waste land. But what of Allie himself? His death from leukemia, three years before, reaped a sterile harvest: D. B. sacrificed his "goldfish" for the movies; Holden crippled his hand on the garage windows—and one side of his head turned gray. Like Seymour, Allie remains in spirit as the essence of truth and innocence. It is only to the degree that Holden can see the spirit of the saintly Allie in humanity that he can forgive those who do not conform to his ideal; that he can become his own savior as well as a savior of others.

II. STRUCTURE

The Burial of the Dead

Before leaving Pencey, Holden goes to see Mr. Spencer, his history teacher, who initially resembles Eliot's Madame Sosostris in that both have bad colds which interfere greatly with their prophetic powers. Madame Sosostris tells the hero's fortune with a "wicked pack" of Tarot cards—associated historically with Egypt. Spencer tells Holden's fortune with his poorly answered examination on the Egyptians; all Holden can remember is how they bury their dead: "Modern science would still like to know what the secret ingredients were that they Egyptians used when they wrapped up dead people with so that their faces would not rot for innumerable centuries. This interesting riddle is still quite a challenge" (p. 14).

Holden, who has just that morning lost the fencing team's foils, is told that "Life is a game" (p. 11); and later asked: "Do you feel absolutely no concern for your future, boy?" (p. 6). But the "boy" is, at this moment, thinking about the frozen lagoon, and wondering where the ducks go in the winter; all he knows is: "I didn't like hearing him say that. It made me sound dead or something" (p. 17).

Appropriately, Holden lives in the "Ossenburger Memorial Wing of the new dorms" (p. 18), named after an undertaker, a wealthy and hypocritical alumnus. Eliot's quester makes a grotesque joke with the character Stetson: "That corpse you planted last year in your garden./Has it begun to sprout? Will it bloom this year?" (KK. 71-72). (Eliot is referring to a hanged God-Christ, Attis, or Osiris, probably the latter.) A parallel is suggested when Holden says that Ossenburger "probably dumps them [the corpses] into the river," and talks "to Jesus all the time" (p. 18). The parallel is extended when Holden says that he talks to Allie (pp. 90, 178), who is "planted," but significantly vulnerable to water in Holden's mind: "twice—*twice*—we were there when it started to rain. It was awful. It rained on his lousy tombstone, and it rained on the grass on his stomach. It rained all over the place. All the visitors that were visiting the cemetery started running like hell over to their cars. That's what nearly drove me crazy...I know it's only his body and all that's in the cemetery, and his soul's in Heaven and all that crap, but I couldn't stand it anyway. I just wish he wasn't there" (p. 141). Significantly, the only other corpse which Holden agonizes over is that of James Castle, who *falls* out a window while Holden "was in the *shower* and all, and...could hear him land outside" (p. 153). Four years later Zooey says that there "*isn't anyone out there who isn't Seymour's Fat Lady*" and that the "Fat Lady" is "Christ Himself..." (p. 200). In *The Catcher* Salinger has apparently chosen to dramatize a similar equation between Holden's "Allie" (Allah?) and James Castle ("J. C."?); that is, "Allie" is "Christ Himself."

A Game of Checkers

Like Holden, Jane Gallagher, one of the few "unphony" people in the book, is poor at games—specifically, the game of checkers, because she insists on keeping her kings in the back row (p. 32). Carl F. Strauch suggests that "the symbolism of this imagery, portraying defense against sexual attack, is the central motif of the episode."[10] Extending this analogue to Holden, he says, "like Jane's kings in the back row, Holden's private world is impotent, and the effort at self-revelation in the theme is of a piece with his futility. His rapidly worsening neurotic condition has frozen him in this posture of feebleness" (p. 14). My immediate concern here is with Jane's obvious similarity to Eliot's lady in *The Waste Land*, who reflects both fear and lust as she plays "A Game of Chess." In this same section, we find allusions to the bewitched Prince Ferdinand, later identified with Phlebas the Phoenician, the "Death by Water" figure, and with Tiresias, the helpless "seer" of degeneration. Significantly, Holden, who tells us that he calls "people a 'prince' quite often when horsing around" (p. 25), pulls his red hat down over his eyes: "I started groping around in front of me, like a blind guy, but without getting up or anything. I kept saying, "Mother darling, why won't you give me your *hand*?" (p. 23). But, like Eliot's blinded heroes and Fisher King, Holden is caught in the "back row" of life; and it is at this point in the story that both his quest and his "fortunate fall" begin. With red hat on head, and Allie's "gauntlet" symbolically in hand, Holden sets out into the waste land, wounded in both spirit and body.

Notes

1. Quoted by Herschel Brickell in "Backstage with Esquire," *Esquire*, XXIV (October 1945), 34.

2. See William Maxwell's brief account of this event in "J.D. Salinger," *Book-of-the-Month Club News*, Midsummer, 1951, p. 6.

3. *Cosmopolitan*, CXXIII (December 1947), 115.

4. New York: Signet Books, p. 156.

5. "J.D. Salinger: 'Some Crazy Cliff' Indeed," *WHR*, XIV (Winter, 1960), 98.

6. Garden City, N.Y.: Anchor Books, 1957, p. 126.

8. *Nine Stories*, p. 116.

9. *Franny and Zooey* (New York, 1961), p. 175.

10. "Kings in the Back Row: Meaning Through Structure—A Reading of Salinger's *The Catcher in the Rye*," *Wisconsin Studies in Contemporary Literature*, II (Winter, 1961), 13.

WARREN FRENCH ON HOLDEN'S SEARCH FOR TRANQUILITY

To determine the exact relationship to an overall pattern of each detail in the novel would require a book as long as the novel itself. It is possible, however, to provide a more complete structural analysis of *The Catcher in the Rye* than has previously appeared by outlining the three main patterns that must be considered in interpreting the work.

Although *Catcher* is richly and elaborately embellished, it is basically the account of the breakdown of a sixteen-year-old boy. The novel does not attempt to trace the whole history of this catastrophe from its origins, but concentrates on the events of its critical stage. Salinger tries hard to make clear just what he is doing when he has Holden comment that "all that David Copperfield kind of crap" bores him and that he is going to tell only "about this madman stuff" that happened just before he got "pretty run-down" (3).*

Even though Holden acknowledges being attended by a psychoanalyst at the end of the book, his breakdown is clearly not just—or even principally—mental. He is physically ill. He has grown six and a half inches in a year and "practically got T.B." (8). He also admits that he is "skinny" and has not kept to the diet that he should to gain weight (140). He is passing through the most physically difficult period of adolescence when only the most sympathetic care can enable the body to cope with the changes it is undergoing.

Holden's condition is complicated, however, by emotional problems. His mother is ill and nervous, and his father is so busy being successful he never discusses things with his son

(140). Holden is thus without the kind of parental guidance an adolescent urgently needs during this crucial period. The school to which he has been packed off fails to take the place of his parents. Holden's complaint is not that Pencey Prep-like schools in European novels such as Sybille Bedford's *A Legacy* or even the monstrous American military academy in Calder Willingham's *End As a Man*—is overbearing or destructive of individuality, but rather that "they don't do any damn more molding at Pencey than they do at any other school" (4). While the administrators entertain prospective donors, the kind of cliques of hoodlums that drive James Castle to suicide operate unchecked. Although Holden is trying to cling to an unrealistically rigid Victorian moral code, he also lacks what David Riesman calls the "psychological gyroscope" that keeps the "inner-directed" personality on course. (To classify Holden in the terms provided by *The Lonely Crowd*, he is an inner-directed" personality in an "other-directed" society—an unhappy phenomenon so common today that it alone could account for many persons' identification with Holden.

Holden also has the intellectual problem of preparing himself for a vocation, because he rejects the kind of career for which his schooling is preparing him and as yet he can conceive of no realistic substitute for it. His emotional and intellectual problems do not, however, cause his breakdown; rather his rundown physical condition magnifies the pain these problems cause him. They boy is struggling, without enlightened assistance, against greater odds than he can fight for himself, and his "quest" during the critical period described in the book is not really for some metaphysical "grail" but simply for a "nice" (he uses the word himself at the end of his adventures, p. 275) refuge from the "phony" world that threatens to engulf him.

Those who find the book nothing more than a satirical attack upon the "phoniness" that irritates Holden's condition are probably as disturbed as the boy himself; for—as Marc Rosenberg points out—Holden suffers because of an undisciplined hypersensitivity.[1] The most common complaint that cooler and supposedly wiser heads like Ernest Havemann[2] level at the novel is that Holden is himself guilty of all the things that make him call other "phony." As Christopher Parker admits, the charge is absolutely true.[3] In the opening chapters of the novel, Salinger strains to make it clear that Holden does precisely what he objects to other people's doing. He displays the vain irresponsibility that he criticizes in "secret slob" Stradlater (35) when he loses the fencing team's equipment (6). He stands in another's light as he complains Ackley does (40,28). He lectures Ackley in the same way that he objects to the history teacher's lecturing him (32, 16-17). Like Ackley, he will do what others want only when he is shouted at (32,63). Like Luce, he will discuss only what he feels like talking about (188, 71). he is especially guilty of overgeneralizing. Although he complains that everybody—especially his father—"think something's all true" when it's only partly true, he ends the very paragraph in which he makes this charge with his own generalization that "people never notice anything" (13). Elsewhere he comments—to cite only a few examples—"people never believe you" (48), women always leave bags in the aisle (70), "all those Ivy League bastards look alike" (112).

There is no point in multiplying examples, Holden obviously fails to see that his criticisms apply to himself. If, however, we think that his failure to practice what he preaches invalidates his criticisms, we fall into an *argumentum ad hominem*—we cannot justify our shortcomings by pointing the finger of scorn at our critics, especially if we do not wish to admit that we are as sick as they are. Like many sensitive but immature people, Holden is not yet well enough in control of his faculties to see the application of his strictures to himself. As Ihab Hassan warns, there is a great a danger "in taking Holden at his word as in totally discounting his claim."[4] Despite Martin Green's claims, Salinger is not offering Holden to the world as an example of what it should be.[5] If those who think that Holden could pull himself together if he would just "try" are as insensitive as the people who fail Holden in the novel, those who make a martyr of Holden are victims of the same immature hypersensitivity that he is. Both make the mistake of supposing that the novel is what Ernest Jones calls "a case history of all of us." It is not; there are adolescents like those Holden says are "as sensitive as a goddam toilet seat" (72); there are those who are driven to suicide by their real or imagined tormentors (like James Castle or Seymour Glass); and there are sensitive ones who are saved by a stronger sense of "inner direction" than Holden possesses. The popularity of the novel suggests, however, that fully literate youth in our society finds it especially easy to identify with Holden.

Many people who read too much of themselves into the novel do not seem to realize that Holden is not seeking admiration, but the understanding that will help him through a difficult period. (When Phoebe does dramatically show admiration for him by insisting upon running away with him, he realizes that he cannot accept the responsibility of hero-worship.) He is not—like most restless rebels in American literature (Leatherstocking, Ahab, Carol Kennicott, Arrowsmith, Clyde Griffiths, Danny in *Tortilla Flat*, Dean Moriarity, Henry Miller in *Tropic of Cancer*, even Nick Carraway, until he is disillusioned)—seeking to run away from a monotonous, humdrum life, but to run toward some kind of tranquil sanctuary. It has not even been generally observed that Holden does not even consider "running away' from urban society until very near the end of the book, and that he leaves school early and goes to New York City so that he can hibernate in a cheap hotel room and "go home all rested up and feeling swell" (66). He cannot carry out this plan, however, because he cannot stand being alone; he feels like "giving somebody a buzz" as soon as he hits town. If he were not constantly seeking company, he might have to think about his situation and his experiences, but he is not yet ready to accept this demanding intellectual responsibility.

He needs sympathy, and he has not been able to find it at school. His history instructor lectures him about things he already knows, but he cannot answer the one question that Holden plaintively asks—"Everybody goes through phases and all, don't they?" (21). His schoolmates aggravate his condition: Ackley will move only if yelled at; Stradlater is not interested in a person's "lousy childhood", but only "very sexy stuff" (42). Both give Holden "a royal pain" by running down the few accomplishments that may give other people some vitally needed self-confidence (37). When Holden yells, "*Sleep tight, ya morons!*" as he leaves Pencey (68), he probably does not fully understand his own motives, but he senses that those he leaves behind are sleeping morons because they are too obsessed with their own nose drops, pimples, and good looks even to be interested in trying to figure out what may really be troubling a boy who they know is flunking out. (Holden, of course, does not try to figure out what their problems are, but he is at least sometime aware that he does not know all about people. His immediate problem, furthermore, is more urgent than theirs.)

Notes

* Figures in parentheses throughout this chapter refer to page numbers in the original edition of *The Catcher in the Rye* (Boston: Little Brown, 1951). This same pagination is preserved in the undated Modern Library edition and also in the Grosset and Dunlap reprint.

1. Warren French with Marc Rosenberg, "The Beast that Devours Its Young," *CCC: The Journal of the Conference on Composition and Communication*, XIII, 7 (May, 1962).

2. Ernest Havemann, "The Search for the Mysterious J.D. Salinger," *Life* (November 3, 1961), p. 141.

3. Grunwald, *Salinger*, p. 255

4. *Ibid*, p. 151

5. *Ibid*., p. 252

DUANE EDWARDS ON HOLDEN AS THE UNRELIABLE NARRATOR

It's not difficult to understand why readers have ignored, or have failed to perceive, Holden's grave deficiencies as a person. After all, he is very appealing—on the surface. He genuinely appreciates brief and isolated instances of kindness and accurately pinpoints phoniness in both high and low places; he is witty and his love for Phoebe is touching. But he himself is a phony at times, and he has virtually no self-awareness. Offered good advice by the psychoanalyst Wilhelm Stekel (through Mr. Antolini), he becomes "so damned *tired* all of a sudden" and is unable to concentrate (188).[4] Confronted with the charge that he cannot name one "thing" he likes "a lot," he again cannot "concentrate too hot" (169). Of course he can't; he's too busy repressing the truth. So he rambles on about two nuns he met briefly and will never see again, and he tries to convince Phoebe—and himself—that he likes James Castle, a boy who is dead. But he cannot name one *living* person, or even one occupation, that he likes. Nevertheless, he believes he is a lover of people in general because he wants to be the catcher in the rye.

When Holden says that he wants to be the catcher in the rye, he reveals a great deal about himself—a great deal more than he knows. He reveals that he does not seriously want to learn about himself. He simply won't make the effort. After all, he hasn't bothered to read Burn's poem; he isn't even able to quote accurately the one line he heard a small boy recite (173); he doesn't know that Burns's narrator contemplates kissing the "body" he meets in the rye field. So when Holden changes the word "meet" to "catch"[5] and talks not of love but of potential death (falling off a cliff), he reveals his willingness to distort the truth by ignoring—or even changing—the facts. He also reveals his use of displacement: he substitutes one response for another. He focuses on danger and potential death instead of love and a personal relationship. Ultimately, he reveals his unreliability as the narrator of his own life's story.

Fortunately, the fact hat Holden distorts doesn't matter to anyone concerned with the significance of the events and dialogue recorded in *The Catcher in the Rye*. Like the psychoanalyst analyzing a dream, the reader can analyze what maters most: the distortions. What emerges from this analysis is an awareness that Salinger's narrator is ironic: he doesn't understand (or know) himself, but he unwittingly lets the reader know what he is like. In fact, he does so at the very beginning of the novel when he promises to give the reader "none of that David Copperfield crap" about his "lousy childhood" (1).[6] Normally, such a statement would be innocent and unrevealing, but Holden isn't "normal"; he's a severely depressed adolescent telling the story of his youth while in a mental institution. He is, by his own admission, sick (213).[7] So his refusal to talk about the incidents of his childhood signifies that he will remain ill, as does his chilling advice, "Don't ever tell anybody anything," at the end of the novel (214).

Elsewhere in the novel there is evidence that Holden will remain ill because he refuses to assume responsibility for his own actions. For example, when he is "the goddam manager of the fencing team," he leaves the "foils and equipment and stuff" on the subway. Although he admits that he left them there, he listens to add: "It wasn't all my fault" (3).[8] Here and elsewhere he simply will not or can not let his mind rest without ambivalence or qualification on a conclusion.

Ambivalence is, in fact, characteristic of Holden and the surest evidence of his mental instability. If he loathes what he loves and does so intensely, he is by no means well. He is also not what he and many readers assume he is: an anti-establishment figure whose disgust is directed entirely at other people. It's easy in to demonstrate that Holden is ambivalent since he is ambivalent toward so many people and things. He hates movies and the Lunts but attends movies (137) and takes Sally to a play starring the Lunts (125). He is contemptuous of Pencey but is careful to emphasize that it has a "very good academic rating" (4). He claims to loathe the perverts he sees through his hotel window but makes a special effort to watch them and even admits that "that kind of junk is fascinating" and that he wouldn't mind doing it himself "if the opportunity came up" (62).[9] He criticizes phony conversations but engages in them himself—with Mr. Spencer (8) and Ernest Morrow's brother (54-55), for example. He criticizes "old Spencer" (and others) for using a phony word like "grand" (9), but he himself uses equally phony words such as "nice" (1) and "swell" (124).[10] He loathes Ackley and Stradlater but misses them as soon as they're gone. He wants to see people—Mr. Antolini, Mr. Spencer, and Carl Luce, for example—but doesn't like them when they're in his presence. Obviously, then, Holden is ambivalent, and ambivalence is a certain indication of mental instability.

What is Holden's problem? Whatever it is in specific form, it's reflected in his inability to relate sexually to females. Holden himself suggests this when he says, "My sex life stinks" (148). But even when he speaks the truth he fools himself: he believes that he cannot "get really sexy" with girls he doesn't like a lot whereas, in reality, he cannot get sexy with a girl he does like. In fact, what he likes about Jane Gallagher is that a relationship with her will not go beyond the hand-holding stage. In his other attempts to establish connections with girls or women, he fails sexually and, in fact, deliberately avoids both affection and serious sexual advances.[11] He kisses Sally Hayes—but in a cab where the relationship cannot go beyond "horsing around" (125). He consents to have a prostitute sent to his hotel room but asks her to stop when she starts "getting funny, Crude and all" (97), that is, when she proceeds from words to action. Aroused by watching the "perverts" in the hotel, he does call up Faith Cavendish (64), a woman he has never seen, but at an impossibly late hour and so ensures that she will refuse his request for a date. Clearly, Holden has a problem with females.

This problem is reflected in his response to Mercutio in *Romeo and Juliet*. Acting in character, Holden identifies with Mercutio, the character in the play he has most in common with. As Strauch has pointed out,[12] both Holden and Mercutio are associated with foils. But the two have much more in common than weapons. To begin with, Mercutio assigns the role of lover to Romeo (I.iv.17) just as Holden assigns the role of lover to Stradlater. Then, too, both young men ramble on when they talk. Mr. Antolini reminds us that this is true of Holden (183 ff.); Romeo calls Mercutio's long speech (I.iv.53-94) "nothing" and Mercutio himself admits that he talks of dreams / Which are the children of an idle brain, / Begot of nothing but vain fantasy" (I.iv.96-98). Finally, both Mercutio and Holden like to "horse around." Holden does so repeatedly; Mercutio does so even when he's dying.

Notes

4. Page numbers which appear parenthetically in the body of this paper refer to the Bantam Books paperback edition of *The Catcher in the Rye*.

5. It's possible that the little boy quoted Burns's poems inaccurately and that Holden is repeating accurately what he heard. Nevertheless, my central point remains valid: Holden is not concerned enough about the truth to gather the facts. Being in the right is much more important to him than being right.

6. In one sense, Holden keeps his promise; he doesn't tell the reader much about his childhood. However, since he reveals his "symptoms" through his speech and behavior, it's possible to infer what his childhood was like. Besides, Holden has something in common with David Copperfield; he's very sentimental. This should surprise no one since Salinger carefully links Holden to David in two ways. First of all, Holden is a Caulfield and David is a Copper-field. Secondly, both are born with a caul. Caul is the first part of Holden's surname, it is also the name of the fetal membrane David is born with (see the fourth paragraph of Dickens' novel).

7. Unwittingly, he acknowledges this again when he says, "In my mind, I'm probably the biggest sex maniac you ever saw" (62). On other occasions he calls himself an exhibitionist (29) and admits that he can be sadistic (22).

8. The significant word here is "all"; it suggests that Holden knows he is at fault but will not assume responsibility for his actions.

9. Carl F. Strauch cites this scene to confirm that Holden contrasts the world be loathes; however, Strauch ignores the fact that Holden finds the perverse behavior attractive. In addition to admitting that indulging in perverse behavior would be "quite a lot of fun," Holden renders a long, detailed account of the women's clothing used by the transvestite (61); he also watches the "perverts" willingly, with obvious interest, and for quite a long time.

10. Holden's use of what Strauch calls "slob" and "literate" language suggests that Holden's ambivalent toward language and toward education in general.

11. It is important to emphasize that Holden has difficult expressing himself either affectionately or sensually. (Sentimentality should not be mistaken for affection.) For example, he finds even Phoebe "too affectionate" when she puts her arms around his neck (161). This inability to express or receive affection suggests that Holden had difficult "from the very beginning" with parents who were to cold or too aloof Since "normal" sexual development depends on the successful fusion of the earlier "affectionate current" of love with the later "sensual current," Holden's chances of maturing "normally" are not good.

12. Strauch, p. 15.

Now that over a quarter century has passed since the publication of *The Catcher in the Rye*, it is possible to see the book in the light of the enormous body of writing that has been done on it. There are collections of articles and bibliographies to aid the person who wishes to do this.[1] It is also possible to see the book in the context of Salinger's other work, especially the writings about the Glass family, most of which were published after *Catcher*. These stories reveal themes not immediately apparent in a reading of *Catcher* and stem from a side of Salinger that has been of less importance to his critics than to Salinger himself. I refer to the importance of Eastern thought and religion to Salinger, and of Buddhism in particular, especially the form which we in the West refer to as Zen.[2]

The Zen masters have a saying, "Sometimes we go east, sometimes we go west," and it appears that Salinger, after a brief attempt to "go west" in the American army during World War II, became disillusioned with his native culture and society and turned to a study of Eastern thought. This disillusionment can be seen in Holden's approving remark about his brother D.B.: "My brother D.B. was in the Army for four goddam years. He was in the war, too—he landed on D-Day and all—but I really think he hated the Army worse than the War...He said the Army was practically as full of bastards as the Nazis were." Of course I don't mean to identify Salinger with D.B., but like D.B. Salinger himself participated in the Normandy invasion and his story, "For Esme—with Love and Squalor," embodies the vision which Holden attributes to D.B.

In Buddhism one is asked to give up one's illusions. *Catcher* was given final shape in the post-war period, and it is basically a novel of disillusionment. The radical nature of Salinger's portrayal of disappointment with American society, so much like Twain's in *Huck Finn*, was probably as much of the reason that *Catcher* (like *Huck*) was banned from schools and colleges as were the few curse words around which the battle was publicly fought.

(...)

Since Salinger seemed to achieve instant success with the appearance of Catcher in 1951, it is important to remember that he was already in his early thirties by this time, had been publishing stories in slick magazines like *Saturday Evening Post* for ten years, and had been working on *Catcher* through much of this decade during which time he was studying Buddhism and working on the beginnings of the Glass family saga as well. ("A Perfect Day for Bananafish," and "*Down at the Dinghy*," were published before *Catcher*).

The Buddha, like most great ancient religious teachers, now exists at the point where the lines of history and legend cross. But as Christmas Humphreys observes in his study of Buddhism, "Legend is often a poetic form of history..."[3] A Raja of the Sakya clan (he is sometimes referred to as Sakyamuni—the sage of the Sakyas), the Buddha, according to tradition, was born in what is now Nepal in 563 B.C. His name was Siddhartha Gotama. Raised in a protective, affluent environment, the young prince was shielded from the suffering of the world and not taught to deal with it. The turning point in the story of the Buddha's life occurs when he is confronted with old age, sickness, and death. They so shake him he decides to leave the shelter of his surroundings and the distractions of his involvement in his everyday life in order to wander in the world in search of a guide who will teach him to come to terms with old age, sickness, and death. He doesn't find one, is forced to work out his salvation on his own, persists in his detachment and alienation, has a vision of the truth, and returns to the world out of compassion for his fellow living suffering beings.

I would suggest that, in rough outline, and without the Buddha's final conscious mature understanding, this is the form of the story of Holden Caulfield. When we first meet Holden in the affluent, protective environment of a prep school, we are prepared for his lonely journey by immediately being given a picture of his alienation from the non-seeing groups of people around him. (Alienation is the negative side of detachment or non-attachment which the Eastern religions see as a virtue.) Salinger presents us with our first glimpse of Holden on the day of the big football game. Holden's detachment from the game is emphasized by having him view the stadium from a distance where the excitement and involvement of the crowd over "the two teams bashing each other all over the place" appears ridiculous. Holden comments, "The game with Saxon Hall was supposed to be a very big deal around Pencey. It was the last game of the year and you were supposed to commit suicide or something if old Pencey didn't win."

The reference to suicide is not fortuitous for we soon come to see that it is precisely a continuing preoccupation with death that keeps Holden from participating in the games of those around him. It prevents him from concentrating on these activities like day-to-day school chores which we don't ordinarily think of as games but which, in the presence of death, tend to recede toward the unimportance we usually ascribe to games.

And, in fact, just as in the story of the Buddha, it is sickness, old age, and death, which we the readers, along with Holden, encounter when we begin our journey though the pages of *The Catcher in the Rye*. We meet sickness and old age in the form of Mr. Spencer, Holden's teacher:

> The minute I went in, I was sort of sorry I'd come. He was reading the *Atlantic Monthly*, and there were pills and medicine all over the place, and everything smelled of Vicks Nose Drops. It was pretty depressing. I'm not too crazy about sick people, anyway. What made it even more depressing, Old Spencer had on this very sad, ratty old bathrobe that he was probably born in or something. I don't much like to see old guys in their pajamas and bathrobes anyway. Their bumpy old chests are always showing. And their legs. Old guys' legs, at beaches and places, always look so white and unhairy.

Holden explains to Mr. Spencer that his problem relates to the idea of life as a game. "He [Dr. Thurmer—the headmaster] just kept talking about life being a game and all." To which "old" Spencer responds, "Life *is* a game, boy." Holden agrees with him outwardly, but he tells us, his confidants, "Game my ass. Some game." At this point Holden believes his objection to life as "a game" is that it's only fun for the winners. But he has deeper, unconscious objections to life, since ultimately in life there are no winners, only corpses. And immediately after introducing sickness and old age, Salinger presents us with the third member of the Buddha's problematic triad—death.

Holden, like the young Buddha, is obsessed by death, and by its corollaries, time and change. He has turned Spencer's exam question about ancient Egypt into a short essay which Spencer cannot see as springing out of this obsession: "Modern science would still like to know what the secret ingredients were that the Egyptians used when they wrapped up dead people so that their faces would not rot for innumerable centuries." And Holden flunks, because on this exam, as in his life, no one has ever taught him how to get beyond this primary question, in the shrill light of which all secondary questions are obscured.

From the start, Holden's mind has been filled with images of rot and decay. (Besides "old" Spencer himself, we have also met his rotting bathrobe.) An it is this obsessive concern of Holden's which accounts for the concentration of his narrative upon details of bodily functioning, dirt, and decay—filthy fingernails, mossy teeth, smelly socks, and rusty, filthy razor—which our institutions attempt to repress or deny.

Disgust is our culturally conditioned response to these natural data, and when the book appeared many teachers and reviewers—people who are successfully functioning within the culture's institutional system—did, in fact, respond to the mention of these matters in the text with disgust. Holden is also disturbed by much of this. He, too, has been raised in this culture (many critics have pointed out that he still holds some of the middle-class values he attacks) and he is sickened by their presence. Yet he can not sweep the evidence of decay and death under the carpet of his mind into his unconscious. He doesn't like what he sees, but he can't help seeing it, just as he can't avoid the presence of the central fact of his life, his brother Allie's death, which ultimately sets him off on his quest for an adult guide.

Salinger himself has his present narrator, Buddy Glass, define the artist as seen, and Buddy too seems determined to wrestle openly with death; not only Holden, but the Glass children as well are obsessed by the death of a brother. It was probably a fight against allowing the facts of death and change to get out of his sight and become unconscious that led Salinger to his post-war studies of such philosophies as Taoism and Buddhism which begin with the primary fact of impermanence and change and attempt to teach us to see and accept this central datum of our experience.

Holden has no one to teach him how to cope with death. In a stable culture, one would ordinarily turn to the oldest people for this kind of wisdom. They've been around the longest and presumably would have had the most experience with these matters. But in a rapidly changing culture like ours, the old people and their knowledge appear obsolete to the young. To Holden, the older people he meets are generally all right, but they seem "out of it": "I have this grandmother that's quite lavish with her dough. She doesn't have all her marbles anymore—she's old as hell..." and in "old" Spencer's case, "he was a nice old guy that didn't know his ass from his elbow."

Seeking protection himself, Holden is forced to protect the adults he encounters. He forgives Spencer in advance for failing him, writing on his exam, "it is all right with me if you flunk me..." Several critics have noted the contradiction between Holden's hatred of phoniness and his lying to Ernest Morrow's mother when he meets her on the train on his way to New York from Pencey. Yet he lies to her to protect her from having to face the fact that "Her son was doubtless the biggest bastard that ever went to Pencey...." And it is interesting that when he lies to her about his name, he doesn't do it for the usual reason one lies—to aggrandize oneself—but rather he takes on the name of Rudolph Schmidt, the dorm janitor.

Notes

1. See the articles in *Salinger*, Henry Anatole Grunwald, ed. (New York Harper and Row, 1962), and *Studies in J. D. Salinger*, Marvin

Laser and Norman Frutman, ads. (New York: The Odyasey Press, 1963), the articles and bibliography in *Salinger's "Catcher in the Rye"*, —*Clamor vs. Criticism*, ed. Harold P. Simonson and Phillip E. Hager (Lexington, Mass.: D. C. Heath, 1963), and the bibliography in Warren French, *J. D. Salinger* (New Haven: College and University Press, 1963).

2. Several critics touch upon this briefly, some with condescension. There are exceptions however, one of which is Tom Davis, "J. D. Salinger: "Some Crazy Cliff Indeed." *Western Humanities Review*, 14 (Winter 1960), 97-99.

3. Christmas Humphrey's, *Buddhism* (Harmondsworth, England: Penguin, 1951), 30.

EDWIN HAVILAND MILLER ON MOURNING ALLIE CAULFIELD

Although J.D. Salinger's *Catcher in the Rye* deserves the affection and accolades it has received since its publication in 1951, whether it has been praised for the right reasons is debatable. Most critics have tended to accept Holden's evaluation of the world as phony, when in fact his attitudes are symptomatic of a serious psychological problem. Thus instead of treating the novel as a commentary by an innocent young man rebelling against an insensitive world or as a study of a youth's moral growth, [1] I propose to read *Catcher in the Rye* as the chronicle of a four-year period in the life of an adolescent whose rebelliousness is his only means of dealing with his inability to come to terms with the death of his brother. Holden Caulfield has to wrestle not only with the usual difficult adjustments of the adolescent years, in sexual, familial and peer relationships; he has also to bury Allie before he can make the transition into adulthood.[2]

Life stopped for Holden on July 18, 1946, the day his brother died of leukemia. Holden was then thirteen, and four years later—the time of the narrative—he is emotionally still at the same age, although he has matured into a gangly six-foot adolescent. "I was sixteen then," he observes concerning his expulsion from Pencey Prep at Christmas time in 1949, "and

I'm seventeen now, and sometimes I act like I'm about thirteen."[3]

On several occasions Holden comments that his mother has never gotten over Allie's death, which may or may not be an accurate appraisal of Mrs. Caulfield, since the first-person narrative makes it difficult to judge. What we can deduce, though, is that it is an accurate appraisal of Holden's inability to accept loss, and that in his eyes his mother is so preoccupied with Allie that she continues to neglect Holden, as presumably she did when Allie was dying.

The night after Allie's death Holden slept in the garage and broke "all the goddam windows with my fist, just for the hell of it. I even tried to break all the windows on the station wagon we had that summer, but my hand was already broken and everything by the time, and I couldn't do it. It was very stupid thing to do, I'll admit, but I hardly didn't even know I was doing it, and you didn't know Allie" (p. 39). The act may have been "stupid"—which is one of his pet words to denigrate himself as well as others—but it also reflects his uncontrollable anger at himself for wishing Allie dead and at his brother for leaving him alone and burdened with feelings of guilt. Similarly, the attack on the station wagon may be seen as his way of getting even with a father who was powerless either to save Allie or to understand Holden. Because he was hospitalized, he was unable to attend the funeral, to witness the completion of the life process, but by injuring himself he received the attention and sympathy which were denied him during Allies illness. His actions here as elsewhere are inconsistent and ambivalent, but always comprehensible in terms of his reaction to the loss of Allie.

So too is Holden's vocabulary an index to his disturbed emotional state—for all that it might seem to reflect the influence of the movies or his attempts to imitate the diction of his older brother, D.B. At least fifty times, something or somebody *depresses* him—an emotion which he frequently equates with a sense of isolation: "It makes you feel so lonesome and depressed" (p. 81). Although the reiteration of the word reveals the true nature of his state, no one in the novel recognizes the signal, perceiving the boy as a kind of adolescent clown rather than as a seriously troubled youth. As his depression deepens to the point of nervous breakdown, furthermore, Holden—who at some level of awareness realizes that he is falling apart—seeks to obscure the recognition by referring to everything as "crazy" and by facetiously likening himself to a "madman."

"Crap," another word he uses repeatedly, is similarly self-reflective. Although it is his ultimate term of reductionism for describing the world, like "crazy" it serves to identify another of his projections. He feels dirty and worthless, and so makes the world a reflection of his self-image. Similarly, if he continually assets, almost screams, that the phony world makes him want to "puke," it is because Holden's world itself has turned to vomit. In his troubled, almost suicidal state he can incorporate nothing, and, worse, he believes there is nothing for him to incorporate. In turn, the significance of his repeated use of variations on the phrase "that killed me" becomes almost self-evident: reflecting his obsession with death, it tells the unsuspecting world that he wishes himself dead, punished and then reunited with Allie.

Although his consistently negative and hostile language thus reflects Holden's despair and is his way of informing the world of his plight, if no one listens it is primarily his own fault. For with the usual fumbling of the hurt he has chosen a means which serves his purposes poorly. While his language may serve to satisfy his need to act out his anger, at the same time it serves to isolate and to punish him further. If in his hostile phrases he is calling for help, he makes certain that he does not receive it. Ashamed of his need—a sixteen-year old crying for emotional support—and unable to accept kindness since in his guilt he feels he does not deserve it, Holden is locked into his grief and locked out of family and society.

In this respect, the first paragraph of *Catcher in the Rye* is one of the most deceptively revealing possible. Although Holden, the would-be sophisticate, relegates his familial background to "David Copperfield kind of crap," he talks about little else except his "lousy childhood." Arguing that he will not divulge family secrets so as not to cause pain, and pretending to respect the feelings of his parents, he verbally mutilates them, and in an ugly way, but if he is to suffer, so must they. He retaliates in kind, not in kindness. Yet the aggressive, assertive tone masks a pitiful, agonized call for emotional support and love.

Equally revealing of Holden's problem is his observation, as he stands alone on a hill that cold December, his last day at Pencey Prep looking down at the football field where his classmates are participating collectively in on of the rites of adolescence: "it was cold as a witch's teat, especially on top of that stupid hill" (p. 4). What he wants is the good mother's breast. And why he needs this maternal comfort so much is implicitly suggested when he descends the hill to say good-by to his history teacher, who cannot understand why in answering a question about Egyptian history on an examination Holden should have begun and ended with a description of the preservation of mummies. The teacher cannot know that Holden has no interest in the Egyptians, only in what happened to Allie, and that he cannot focus on ancient history until he has come to terms with his own past. Nor can he know that Holden has misinterpreted a rejection his father's concern for his future, that the boy wants to be at home, and that to accomplish his goal he has failed in four different schools.

But lest one think that this insensitivity is a fault of the older generation, Salinger next portrays the response of one of Holden's peers to the first of a number of roles he will play in his desperate attempt to disguise his obsession with Allie's death, on the one hand, and his need for parental comfort, on the other. Thus when Holden pulls his red hunting cap over his eyes and says histrionically, "I think I'm going blind...Mother darling, everything's getting so *dark* in here.. Mother darling, give me your hand," the response of his classmate is: "You're nuts...for Chrisake, grow up" (pp. 21-22). Ackley cannot know that Holden assumes Allie's red hair when he puts on the red cap, that the simulated blindness is descriptive of Holden's state, or that he uses the script as a (futile) means of asking for the maternal hand that he believes has been denied to him.

If Ackley does not appreciate the extent to which the death of Holden's red-haired brother informs his posturing, even less in his roommate Stradlater aware of the chain of associations that he sets off when he asks Holden to write a composition for him. Unable to write about a "room or a house" Holden writes about Allie's baseball mitt—an object which is a complex version of a child's security blanket, a sacred relic of the living dead, at the same time that it reminds Holden of betrayal. And thus as he writes about the mitt, we learn directly for the first time of Allie's death and of Holden's self-punishing rage.

Notes

1. Holden Caulfield has been called "a lout," a saint, a "sad little screwed-up" neurotic, and a "beatnik Peter Pan," but he serves none of these epithets, positive or negative. The novel has been read as a critique of "the academic and social conformity of its period" (Maxwell Geismar), as a modern version of the Orestes-Iphigeneia story (Leslie Fiedler), as a commentary on the modern world in which ideals "are denied access to our lives" (Thab Hassan), or as a celebration of life (Martin Green). These essays appear in *Salinger—A Critical and Personal Portrait*, ed. Henry Anatole Grunwald (New York, 1962).

2. James Bryan recognizes that "the trauma" behind Holden's problems is the death of his brother Allie, but he proceeds to examine the work in terms of Holden's psychosexual growth when clearly the youth's development is emotionally arrested. See "The Psychological Structure of *The Catcher in the Rye*, PMLA, B9 (1974), 1065-74.

3. J.D. Salinger, *The Catcher in the Rye* (New York, 1964), p. 9.

CHRISTOPHER BROOKEMAN ON CULTURAL CODES AT PENCEY PREP

By turning Holden into a symptom of a general cultural malaise, critics have failed to give attention to the fact that Salinger locates Holden's story within a very specific social world in which the most significant influence is not some generalized concept of American culture of society, but the codes and practices of a particular instrument of social control—the American prep school. Even when the action moves to New York, Holden stays, in the main, within a finely tuned collegiate culture of dates and moviegoing. This is clear from his description of the sociology of the clientele in a Greenwich Village nightclub named after the resident pianist: "Even though it was so late, old Ernie's was jam-packed, mostly with prep school jerks and college jerks."[4] It is within the immediate, primary context of Pencey Prep, where we first encounter Holden, that we need to situate all the agencies that seek to influence his development, such as the peer group. Parents, and the mass media. Only then will we do justice to J.D Salinger's portrait of the anxiety-ridden adolescent within the particular fraction of the middle class whose behavior and psychology are the substance of *The Catcher in the Rye*.

Holden seems to have attended three prep schools: Whooton, Elkton Hills, and Pencey. The character and function of this type of private school is delineated in David Riesman's portrait of such a school in the late 1940s, taken from his companion book to *The Lonely Crowd*, called *Faces in the Crowd* (1952):

> Livingston School, a boys' preparatory school in a small Connecticut town, draws on the top of the social system ... from the East.... Its masters are mostly graduates of Ivy League colleges. ... It is not as old a school as St. Marks ... or as civilized as Choate ... [the masters] look askance at innovation.[5]

The evolution of single-sex boarding schools like St. Mark's and Choate (which John F. Kennedy attended) had a specific function which Holden experiences. In its purest form this kind of school was created in the nineteenth century to educate, socialize, and monitor the male offspring of the professional and business classes. As modern society developed its diverse industrial and administrative systems, such institutions as the church, the ancient universities, and the family began to cede power and responsibility for educating and controlling children to others. Throughout the nineteenth and twentieth centuries the dominant role of the family has been steadily supplanted, though not entirely replaced, by a whole range of institutions such as the school. The college, the firm, and the state bureaucracies. These institutions became places where the young future professionals of the middle and upper classes experienced an extended period of training and socialization.

(...)

Salinger employs two main ways of creating his portrait of the culture of the Eastern prep school as exemplified by the fictional Pencey of Agerstown, Pennsylvania. First there are Holden's invariably debunking assessments of prep school traditions and customs such as the one just quoted. Second there are his extended ritualistic encounters, usually with particular members of the faculty like Spencer, Holden's history teacher at Pencey. These encounters have the character of rituals in that they are repetitive, like exercises or verbal push-ups.; They are Holden's way of keeping in shape. The form of these encounters is usually dialogue, interspersed with personal commentary by Holden.

Holden's commentaries on the value of the system of Pencey Prep lead him to conclude that the whole official vision of the school as a cooperative caring family is a mask for an actual ideology of intense competitive struggle between its individual members and factions. This official image of the prep school as an idealized family standing in loco parentis was a favorite metaphor with the historical culture and discourse of the prep school idea.

(...)

Alongside the image of the family, the prep school promoted the metaphor of life as a fame conducted according to the rules of fair play. Dr. Thurmer, the headmaster of Pence, in his farewell address to Holden when he informs him that he is being thrown out for flunking four subjects and is not applying himself, uses the occasion to impress on Holden that life is a "game" and "you should play it according to the rules." Holden's response, delivered to the reader, is characteristic:

> Game, my ass. Some game. If you get on the side where all the hotshots are, then it's a game; all right— I'll admit that. But if you get on the other side ... then what's a game about it?

Holden's career in the world of team games is limited to that of being manager of the Pencey fencing team. The management of people is a key still in postindustrial America, and Holden signally falls in this area. He loses the team foils and equipment on the subway and is consequently ostracized by the team. However, it would be wrong to see Holden as without sporting skills. He does describe himself as "a very good golfer," good enough to be asked to appear in a golfing movie short. But his personal code and hatred of the Hollywood star system, which seeks to turn al skills into commodities, makes him reject this opportunity to star. Holden turns his back on one of the greatest honors America can offer its citizens, a starring role:

> I almost was once in a movie short, but I changed my mind at the last minute. I figured that anybody that hates the movies as much as I do, I'd be a phony if I let them stick me in a movie short.

Holden's ability to expose and deconstruct the contradictions within the official ideology of Pencey Prep in virtuoso asides, like some latter-day Hamlet, should not blind us to the fact that Holden is also a connoisseur and exploiter of the systems he despises. He is both insider and outsider. Although he has a fantasy of fleeing from civilization like Huck and living in Nature, he is very much the college man-about-town, adept at telephone dating techniques, habitué of nightclubs and hotel lounges, and possessed of that crucial urban skill of riling cab drivers. Admittedly he experiences some spectacular failures, as in the encounter with the prostitute and her pimp, but overall, the sixteen-year old, six-foot, two-inch teenager with a crew cut and red hunting cap cannot be characterized as the eternal gauche outsider. His ability to fathom the mind-sets of his peer group gives him a radar-like awareness of social and psychological messages, often to the point of paralyzing overload. In many ways the burgeoning myth of Holden the sullen outsider obscures the degree to which he is also very gregarious and manipulative. Holden needs other people in order to define himself. He is endless in pursuit of company, calling people on the phone, both acquaintances and strangers, and waylaying his colleagues at Pencey as they are washing or dressing.

Viewed from this perspective, Holden's ritualistic encounters with his peer group are not just bull sessions or adolescent horseplay, but part of Salinger's extremely shrewd contribution to the considerable postwar debate on what was called the changing American social character.... Holden's running commentary on society is an index of his negotiations with these various agencies, which is probably why the book has a cult status among teenagers. It has the quality of a training manual on techniques of survival.

Notes

4. J.D. Salinger, *The Catcher in the Rye* (New York: Bantam, 1964), p. 83. All subsequent references, appearing in parentheses in the text, are to this edition.

5. David Reisman, *Faces in the Crowd* (New Haven: Yale University Press, 1952), p. 282.

SANFORD PINSKER ON THE PROTAGONIST-NARRATOR

Consider, for example, the differences between Holden's narrative stance and one it consciously echoes—namely, the opening salvo of the *Adventures of Huckleberry Finn*: "You don't know abut me, without you have read a book by the name of "The Adventures of Tom Sawyer," but that ain't no matter."[1]Huck is a battered child while Holden has been spoiled rotten. Huck has no illusions about his ignorance while Holden peppers his chatter with SAT words like "ostracized." Perhaps most important of all, while Huck's adventures alter him significantly (he is not the same sucker in the novel's last paragraphs he was throughout his sojourn south), Holden remains essentially the same self-indulgent romantic he always was.

About some similarities, however, there is little doubt. Take, for example, Huck's description of the lynch mob dispersing, tail between its legs, in the face of Colonel Sherburn's hard, courageous speech: "The crowd washed back sudden, and then broke all apart and went tearing off every which way, and Buck Harness he heeled it after them, looking tolerable cheap. I could a staid, if I'd a wanted to, but I didn't want to" (Twain, 126), Salinger gives Holden a similar bit of unconvincing bravado: "Once, at the Whooton School, this other boy, Raymond Goldfarb, and I bought a pint of Scotch and drank it in the chapel one Saturday night, where nobody'd see us. He got stinking, but I hardly didn't even show it. I just got very cool and nonchalant. I puked before I went to bed, but I didn't really have to—I forced myself" (90). In both cases, what amuses is the innocence with which the respective protagonists try to put a good face on what we, as readers, reckon to be embarrassing moments. At the same time, however, even sophisticated readers remember similar episodes from their own lives, and rather than censure Huck or Holden, they are likely to be sympathetic and forgiving.

Much the same thing can be observed about the penchant both protagonists have for the "stretcher," or tall tale. In *Catcher*, we observe Holden's whoppers about his impending death: the "tiny little tumor" on his brain, the imaginary bullet in his gut, a recent operation on his "clavichord," and his deep suspicions that he has many, if not all, the warning signs of cancer. Huck, by contrast, saves up his most inventively gruesome leg-pullers for survival, but as Lionel Teilling pointed out more than forty years ago, he does not lie to himself. One could argue that Holden does precisely that, at least in most of the confrontations between the phony and the pure he reports. As Holden admits at one point, "I'm always saying 'Glad to've met you' to somebody I'm not at *all* glad I met" (87).

Aside from their respective initiations into the variety and the viciousness of adult corruption, Huck and Holden share the mutual condition of being protagonists in death-haunted novels. Hardly a page of either book is spared the taint of mortality, whether it expresses itself in the chivalric rhetoric of the Grangerfords or in Holden's exam essay or Egyptian mummies, in the grisly specter of Buck or in the haunting memories of Allie, in Huck's conviction that "an owl, away off, who-whooing [is] about somebody that was going to die" (Twain, 2), or in Holden's quick leap from a magazine article about the warning signs of cancer to the certainty of the grave: "I'd had this sore on the inside of my lip for about *two* weeks. So I figured I was getting cancer" (196).

Morever, Holden's speech is filled with slang that can be read simultaneously on two levels. When, for example, he points out that this or that "killed him" (usually with reference to the surprising politeness or just plain whimsy of children), the phrase cannot help but call our attention to his brooking obsession with his brother Allie's death, and, indeed, about death in general. And when Phoebe exclaims that "Daddy'll kill you!" because Holden has flunked out of yet another prep school, the point is less that there is an Oedipal struggle going on in the Caulfield's expensive Manhattan apartment than that this is the hyperbolic way adolescents actually speak. Salinger, of course, chooses such words with care—again, not because he has an Oedipal card up his sleeve, but rather because "Daddy'll kill you!" is one strand in a much larger pattern of death imagery. Let me reiterate that unlike the characters in Sophocles' *Oedipus Rex* or in Freud's case histories, Holden harbors no competitive, much less murderous, thoughts toward his father, and the same thing is true about Mr. Caulfield toward Holden.

Beside obsession with death, Huck and Holden also share in the loneliness that stems inextricably from their respective broodings and that is built into their retrospective narratives.

Often in comparable novels like *Moby-Dick*, only Ishmael, the novel's protagonist-narrator, escapes to tell his tale. In other cases like Marlow in *Heart of Darkness* or Nick Carraway in *The Great Gatsby*, the protagonist narrator's experiences have been so traumatic, so fundamentally altering, that they no longer "see" the world as others do.

*The Catcher in the Ry*e, then, fairly aches to be read as an urban twentieth century variant of the *Adventures of Huckleberry Finn*, and while the generalization reduces some important distinctions, those readers who saw Twain's Mississippi reflected on Manhattan's streets were not essentially wrong. The protagonist-narrators of both novels filter experience through their respective sensibilities, make bids for our undivided attention, and, in effect, do what they can to walk off with the whole show. But that much said, there are important differences between Twain's retrospective protagonist and Salinger's. For Huck not only unrolls his tale is a straightforward, chronological fashion, but, more important, he describes far more than he judges. As part of the larger satiric convention that brought the hayseed to the city or Gulliver to the land of the Brobdingagians, Huck's "ignorance" has a decided satiric advantage—for his unqualified admiration of, say, the Grangerfords' house (with its garish mantle clock and fake fruit) or Emmeline Grangerford's god-awful poetry is at once funny and satirical. After all, most readers know bad taste when they see it and bad poetry when they hear it, and can make up for Huck's cultural ignorance by filling in the gaps. Meanwhile, the tragic dimensions of the Adventures of Huckleberry Finn churn just underneath its satiric surface.

By contrast, Holden's story is filled with what his Oral Expression class learned to call "digressions." Rather than proceeding in a straight line, he wanders, first announcing, "I'll just tell you about his madman stuff that happened to me around last Christmas" (1), and then pausing to describe his brother. Granted, Holden's casual leaps and associative jumps come with the territory of adolescence and help to establish his credibility as a seventeen-year-old narrator. But the extended asides also give Salinger an opportunity to move Holden's perchant for hyperbole ("He just got a Jaguar. One of those little English jobs that can do around two hundred miles an hour") to the exaggerated "specialness" that marks Salinger's characters like a thumbprint: "He's got a lot of dough, now. He didn't use to. He used to be just a regular writer, when he was home. He wrote this terrific book of short stories, *The Secret Goldfish*, in case you never heard of him. The best one in it was "The Secret Goldfish." It was about his little kid that wouldn't let anybody look at his goldfish because he'd bought it with his own money. It killed me. Now he's out in Hollywood, D.B., being a prostitute. If there's one thing I hate, it's the movies. Don't even mention them to me" (1-2). No matter that Holden would be quick to censure the *adult* who refused to let anybody look at, say, his hard-earned BMW; no matter that Holden's professed hatred of the movies is suspect—for one who knocks the flicks, he certainly spends a good deal of his time taking them in. The point is that Salinger's protagonist prefers the innocence and secrets of childhood to the world of getting and spending where writers give up goldfish for Hollywood gelt. Thus, D.B. gets written off with a single, judgmental word: prostitute.

Note

1. Mark Twain, *Adventures of Huckleberry Finn* in *Norton Anthology of American Literature*, 3d ed. (New York: W.W. Norton, 1979); hereafter cited in text as Twain.

PAUL ALEXANDER ON INVENTING HOLDEN CAULFIELD

But early in 1941, Salinger had found the subject matter about which he was suppose to write. For some time he had been searching for that special character or milieu; as it is with most writers, much of this process of discovery had been unspoken, even accidental, as if he were going about it by instinct. Then, even though he was only in his early twenties, he came to understand that the vehicle through which he was destined to examine the world in such a way as to make his fiction distinctly his own was Holden Caulfield.

The story was "Slight Rebellion Off Madison," and in it Holden is a kind of teenage Everyman. "While riding on Fifth Avenue buses," Salinger wrote, "girls who knew Holden often thought they saw him walking past Sak's or Altman's or Lord & Taylor's, but it was usually somebody else," Holden is a study in ordinariness, as evidenced by the events documented in the story. He comes home from prep school; kisses his mother; meets his girlfriend, Sally Hayes, for a drink and a night on the town dancing; tells Sally he loves her in the taxi just before she tells him she loves him; and goes with her to the next night to see the Lunts in *O Mistress Mine* on Broadway. This is just the sort of life East Side WASPs raised their children to lead, and from all indications Holden is going to do his part to carry on the lifestyle. It's implied he will finish prep school, go to college, marry Sally Hayes, get a respectable job, buy an appropriate apartment, and have children who will be raised to be like their parents.

Or at least that's what Holden *is suppose to do*. However, Holden is in the middle of an emotional meltdown. Over drinks, he bares his soul to Sally in a long monologue during which he confesses he hates "everything." "I hate living in New York," he says. "I hate the Fifth Avenue buses and Madison Avenue buses and getting out at the center door." That's not all, either. He hates plays, movies, even fitting sessions at Brooks Brothers. So he tells Sally he wants the two of them to leave New York, go to Vermont or "around there," and live in a cabin near a brook until the money he has—one hundred and twelve dollars—runs out. Then he'll get a job up there so they can live in the country. Always the good WASP, Sally cannot begin to understand the motivation behind Holden's "slight rebellion." "You can't just do something like that," she tells him.

The story ends with Holden making a drunken telephone call in the middle of the night to Sally to tell her that he will join her to trim her Christmas tree as planned. Even so, there is a disturbed, and disturbing, quality to the conversation.

Holden's line "Trim the tree for ya," which he repeats over and over like a mantra, has a pleading, desperate quality to it, as if he is asking Sally to give him some sign she still wants him despite what he has told her before. She says what he hopes she will say—yes, she wants him to come trim her tree—but still, that answer doesn't seem to be enough.

By inventing Holden Caulfield, Salinger had entered an arena where he would be able to produce significant fiction. Holden was that genuine article—the literary creation that speaks from the soul of the author to the heart of the reader. Salinger had to realize Holden was special because he started another story about him right away. At this rate, perhaps he would end up with a series of stories about Holden. There was one other fact Salinger knew, and it was important. As Salinger would admit years later, Holden was an autobiographical character. Holden's drunken telephone call to Sally, for example, was based on an episode Salinger himself had lived. In the future Salinger would repeatedly contend that fictitious events had to sound real to the reader. In Salinger's case, he may have ensured that authenticity by basing his characters on real people, himself among them.

Salinger wanted to do something with "Slight Rebellion Off Madison" right away. So, at his urging, Olding submitted the story to the *New Yorker*, and in November, much to Salinger's surprise, the editors accepted it, probably looking to run it right away since the story is set during the Christmas season. When he got word of the acceptance, Salinger was overjoyed. He had been eager to break into the pages of the *New Yorker*; at the amazingly young age of twenty-two, he had been successful. Elated, Salinger wrote to William Maxwell, who would be his editor for this story at the magazine. He had another story about Holden, but he was going to hold off on sending it to him, Salinger said. Instead, Salinger told Maxwell, he would try a different story on him—another one about prep-school children, an obese boy and his two sisters.

As the *New Yorker* prepared to publish "Slight Rebellion Off Madison," the Japanese attacked Pearl Harbor on December 7, 1941, and all warning Roosevelt had made through the years about radical nationalism growing uncontrollably in parts of Europe and Asia seemed more than justified. Within hours, Roosevelt asked Congress, and Congress agreed, to declare war on Japan. The start of war meant the editors of the *New Yorker* did not feel it was appropriate to publish—so soon after Pearl Harbor—a story about a neurotic teenage boy whose "slight rebellion" is prompted by the fact that he has become disenchanted with the life he leads as the son in a wealthy family in New York. Holden's problems were trivial compared to world developments. So the magazine's editors postponed the publication of Salinger's story. Although he would not know it at the time, the editors would not publish "Slight Rebellion Off Madison" until after the conclusion of World War II. It would be years, then, before Salinger realized his dream of seeing his work appear in the magazine he respected most.

However, Salinger had larger concerns than the question of whether the *New Yorker* was going to run his story. At twenty-two, he was prime material for military service. Earlier in 1941, he had tried to join the Army, but military doctors turned him down because he had a minor heart condition. With the United States about to enter a world war, it was only a matter of time before Salinger's heart condition would be considered negligible, making him eligible for the newly sanctioned draft.

PAMELA HUNT STEINLE ON HOLDEN AS A VERSION OF THE AMERICAN ADAM

Looking at contemporary American literature from his 1955 vantage, Lewis identified three novels in the post-World War II period as examples of "the truest and most fully engaged American fiction after the second war": *Invisible Man* by Ralph Ellison, *The Adventures of Augie March* by Saul Bellow, and *The Catcher in the Rye* by J. D. Salinger. Lewis saw each of these novels as among the very few to continue the Adamic fictional tradition of solitary experience and moral priority over the waiting world. He applauded the efforts of these mid-twentieth-century writers as they "engender[ed] from within their work the hopeful and vulnerable sense of life that makes experience and so makes narrative action possible," yet who did so by "creat[ing] it from within, since they can scarcely find it any longer in the historic world about them." [15]

Here, Lewis's recognition of the intersection between his own formulation of the "American Adam" as a once dominant yet recently shrinking force in American culture and the story of Holden Caulfield is the first clue as to the source of cultural tension created by *The Catcher in the Rye*. A story of traditional appeal and yet a contemporary oddness, both fit and lack of fit with the historic dialogue are evident when *Catcher* is examine in light of Lewis's argument.

The classic characterization of the American Adam was he nineteenth-century image of a "radically new personality, the hero of the new adventure," "happily bereft of ancestry," and free of the taint of inherited status to stand alone, "self-reliant and self-propelling, ready to confront whatever awaited him with the aid of his own unique and inherent resources." As the nineteenth century drew to a close, this characterization was modified as American literature reflected concurrent perceptions of social and environmental changes in American life: the movement of the "frontier" from forest to barren plain, and ultimately to closure. The American Adam, no longer situated in an Edenic world, found himself instead "alone in a hostile, or at best a neutral universe." Nevertheless, Lewis claimed that the Adamic character remained intact throughout the first half of the twentieth century, "for much of that fable remained ... the individual going forth toward experience, the inventor of his own character and creator of his personal history." [16]

Bearing these characterizations in mind, at this point I introduce to you Holden Caulfield, as J. D. Salinger did in the first page of *The Catcher in the Rye*:

> If you really want to hear about it, the first thing you'll probably want to know is where I was born, and what my lousy childhood was like, and how my parents were

occupied and all before they had me, and all that David Copperfield kind of crap, but I don't feel like going into it, if you want to know the truth. In the first place, that stuff bores me, and in the second place, my parents would have about two hemorrhages a piece if I told anything personal about them ... Besides, I'm not going to tell you my whole goddam autobiography or anything. I'll just tell you about this madman stuff that happened to me around last Christmas. [17]

In Holden's statement of introduction, his position as a solitary individual in the Adamic tradition is not only evident but reinforced by the contrast to English literary tradition ("that David Copperfield kind of crap"). The initial assumption is that the mid-twentieth-century reader wants to know the family and position of a central character—an assumption that is immediately challenged as irrelevant to the telling of the story itself and as contrary to middle-class expectations of personal and family privacy. Hence, Salinger's introduction of his central character provided an opening defense for the Adamic narrative as well as an implicit jab at the movement of contemporary readers away from that very tradition.

Defense of the Adamic tradition is not surprising in light of Holden's apparent literary lineage. Searching for a fictional representative for his American mythos, "unambiguously treated" and "celebrated in his very Adamism,"[18] Lewis chose James Fenimore Cooper's Natty Bumppo: hero of *The Deerslayer* and, it seems a direct if unacknowledged ancestor of Salinger's Holden Caulfield. In a central scene in *The Deerslayer*, Natty Bumppo's name is changed as the consequence of his fight with a Huron warrior. In their struggle, Natty kills the warrior, but Cooper characterizes it as a chivalrous battle, ending with the dying man telling Natty that he should now be known as "Hawkeye" instead of the boyish "Deerslayer." [19] In this pivotal moment, Natty takes on the heroic status of the American Adam: "born with all due ceremony during an incident that has every self-conscious quality of a ritual trial…[,] Deerslayer earns his symbolic reward of a new name." [20]

If the notion of rebirth is characteristic of the American Adam, it is crucial to the overlapping American narrative of "regeneration through violence" in which acts of violence and destruction are seen as fair practice when they purportedly allow a morally strengthened consciousness to emerge.[21] And it is in keeping with both traditions, then, that early on in *Catcher*, Holden Caulfield purchases a red hunting cap that his prep school roommate calls a "deer-shooting cap." "Like hell it is," Holden retorts, and then clarifies to the reader of his narrative, "I took it off and looked at it. I sort of closed one eye, like I was taking aim at it. "This is a people shooting hat, I said. "I shoot people in this hat"" (22).[22]

Further along, Holden battles an older and stronger classmate to protect the reputation of a female friend and finds himself on the losing end of the fight. Searching for his cap in defeat, Holden comes face-to-face with himself, and it is this critical moment of self-recognition that will lead to his leave-taking of Pencey Prep:

> I couldn't find my goddam hunting hat anywhere. Finally, I found it. It was under the bed. I put it on, and turned the peak around to the back, the way I liked it, and then I went over and took a look at my stupid face in the mirror. You never saw such gore in your life. I had blood all over my mouth and chin and even on my pajamas and bathrobe. It partly scared me and it partly fascinated me. All that blood and all sort of made me look tough. I'd only been in about two fights in my life, and I lost both of them. I'm not too tough. I'm a pacifist, if you want to know the truth. (45)

If the first passage recalls the heroic tradition of Cooper's *Deerslayer* (Holden donning the symbolic garb of the deer hunter and further identifying himself by his hawkeyed aim), then the second passage can be seen as a suggestion for a new errand for the Adamic hero: that of pacifism except when called to the protection of innocents. His ritual battle endured, Holden's reversal of the hunting cap brings to mind the cap of a baseball *catcher*. Holden is thus implicitly renamed and it is a name he will later explicitly claim.

Just as the moment of trial and rebirth was the creation of Lewis's Adamic character, it was his survival through a later "fall" from grace that brought the character to heroic status. Although the consequences of such a fall would entail some suffering, the fall itself offered an opportunity for learning necessary to the character's growth in moral understanding and conscience to fully heroic stature. In the writing of the elder Henry James, for example, the hero "had to fall, to pass beyond childhood in an encounter with "Evil,'" and "had to mature by virtue of the destruction of his own egotism." The very act of "falling" opened the path to moral perfection, a state viewed by James as achievable "not by learning, only by *unlearning*."[23]

Considered within this framework of the "fortunate fall," Holden's experiences after he leaves Pencey Prep can be seen as necessary to his developing moral stature: from his introduction to the seamy side of New York City life via bar flies, stale cabs, hotel pimps and prostitutes to his confrontation with Mr. Antolini.

Notes

15. Ibid., 197, 198.

16. Ibid., 5, 111.

17. J. D. Salinger, *The Catcher in the Rye* (New York: Bantam Books, 1964), 1. Further citations appear parenthetically in the text.

18. Lewis 91

19. See James Fenimore Cooper, *The Deerslayer* (1841; Albany: SUNY P. 1987), 124-29.

20. Lewis 104.

21. See Richard Slotkin, *Regeneration through Violence* (Middletown, Conn.: Wesleyan UP, 1973), and also Richard Drinnon *Facing West: They Metaphysics of Indian-Hating and Empire-Building* (New York: New American Library, 1980).

22. Of note, this section of the novel is interpreted by Alan Nadel in *Containment Culture* as evidence that Holden Caulfield is a fictional McCarthyite: "Donning his red hunting hat, he attempts to become

the good Red-hunter, ferreting out the phonies and subversives" (71). Se my introductory discussion of my disagreement with Nadel's interpretation.

23. Lewis 55, 57.

MATT EVERTSON ON HOLDEN CAULFIELD'S LONGING TO CONSTRUCT A NEW HOME

I'd rather have a goddam horse. A horse is at least *human*, for God's sake.
   —Holden Caulfield, 16, *The Catcher in the Rye*

What he loved in horses was what he loved in men, the blood and the beat of the blood that ran them.
   — John Grady Cole, 16, *All the Pretty Horses*

Shortly after its publication in 1951, critics began comparing the *Catcher in the Rye*, for better or worse, to one of the most important and influential works in the American canon: *Adventures of Huckleberry Finn*. Fifty years later, *The Catcher in the Rye* has become the lodestone to which much contemporary adolescent fiction now points. In the tradition of comparing Holden to Huck, I would argue that the best contemporary candidate to pick up the mantle of *The Catcher in the Rye*—a work that captures the adolescent thrill of running away, the fear of growing up and leaving home, and which lays bare the complex anger of love and death in the lives of young people— is Cormac McCarthy's *All the Pretty Horses*. While little is documented about the influence J. D. Salinger has had on Cormac McCarthy (himself very reclusive, not given to interviews), there are undeniable similarities between each writer's most popular work.[1] *The Catcher in the Rye* was written and takes place in the late 1940s, while *All the Pretty Horses* was published in 1992 but takes place in 1949. McCarthy details the Southwestern and Mexican adventures of sixteen-year-old John Grady Cole during the same period that Holden Caulfield (also sixteen) struggles through his mental and physical collapse in an East Coast metropolis. The titles of both works reference songs of children: a skewed version of the Robert Burns poem sung by a boy on a Sunday morning sidewalk ("If a body *catch* a body coming through the rye") and a traditional children's lullaby ("All the Pretty Little Horses").[2] And while a New Yorker and a Texan might seem to have little in common, Holden Caulfield and John Grady Cole both fantasize about reclaiming a romantic West and escaping the materialistic and selfish adult society that has abandoned them. Even horses mark time in both novels, as the epigraphs above indicate, riding at the core of John Grady's universe (allowing his escape from the oil-boon snags of fresh Texas highways and fencelines) and sidling into city-boy Holden's fantasies of flight, a more "human" answer to the coarse mechanics of Ed Banky's car (especially, its back seat). Both novels offer a dead-aim analysis of the universal condition of growing up, concentrated on the very threshold between the child and adult—with its movement, escape, borders, and barriers on two distinct geographical landscapes and from two distinct historical vantage points—in the same period of what some consider America's own tumultuous "coming of age" (her economic, political, and artistic growth following World War II).

(...)

Taking Control of Taking Off

I put my red hunting hat on, and turned the peak around to the back, the way I liked it, and then I yelled at the top of my goddam voice, "Sleep tight, ya morons!"
—*The Catcher in the Rye*

If I don't go will you go anyways? John Grady sat up and put his hat on. I'm already gone, he said.
—*All the Pretty Horses*

Both *The Catcher in the Rye* and *All the Pretty Horses* begin with escape. In the thrill of running away, however, one forgets that John Grady Cole and Holden Caulfield are homeless, both physically and emotionally, and that sixteen-year-olds wandering the deserted streets at night, be it in Manhattan or Mexico, is in fact a sad circumstance. Forced to take off on their own, these characters remind us of their abandonment— no nurturing parents to embrace them with comforting arms, no reasonable adults to hear their needs and provide for their emotional well-being.

Though born into a life of privilege, Holden hints in the opening pages an emotional poverty in his family life even while refusing to discuss his "lousy childhood" or how his parents were "occupied" before they had him and all the "David Copperfield kind of crap" (3). One of the more powerful image of Holden's isolation is prominently featured in these opening pages, when the reader joins a solitary boy standing on top of Thompson Hill, who has been ostracized for losing the fencing team's gear in the city, looking down upon generations of the "Pencey family" gathered for the traditional football rivalry with Saxon Hall: "you could hear them all yelling, deep and terrific on the Pencey side, because practically the whole school except me was there" (5). Despite the blasé attitude he affects, the scene stresses that Holden at sixteen is a practiced outsider, having already faced a lifetime of upheavals, moved around like one of the checkers he speaks of so reverently in regard to Jane Gallagher (no wonder he admires her impulse to keep her kings safely and predictably at home in the back row). Hanging around for "some kind of a good-by" Holden expresses a desire to control his exile, to stage his exit, and to take his leave on his own terms. "I don't care if it's a sad good-by or a bad good-by," he argues, "but when I leave a place I like to *know* I'm leaving it. If you don't, you feel even worse" (7). When his bloody confrontation with Stradlater hastens his flight, his parting shot to his "moron" prep school companions recasts Holden as misunderstood victim, willing to face a cold night without sure shelter while they insensitively "sleep tight" in their collusion against him. His "decision" to leave, then, subverts the plan to kick him out, delays what can only be an unpleasant return to his parents, and buys him (along with the proceeds of his hawked typewriter) a couple of days on his own in the city.

Despite his posturing towards independence, when Holden first arrives in New York he "accidentally" gives the cab driver the address of his parent's apartment betraying, many critics theorize, his true desire to retreat to his boyhood "home" rather than to hit the town. If he longs to be "welcomed" home, the inevitable anger and disappointment of his parents and the attendant loss of his control and independence keep him on the run. Instead, Holden will try to construct a home built towards his own comfort and control; his sparse and lonely hotel room, however, proves a poor domestic space, and the denizens of New York night life provide little in the way of "family." Finding little companionship with the three young women tourists in the hotel lounge, Holden hails a cab to Greenwich Village. Trying to draw the cabby, Horwitz, into a friendly conversation, he asks if he knows where the ducks in Central Park go in the winter. Horwitz, however, dismisses Holden and argues that the fish in the frozen lake are of more concern than the "stupid" ducks. Joining a long list of incredulous spectators to Holden's attempts to pass as an adult, Horwitz asks "How the hell old are you, anyways?" and "Why ain'tcha home in bed?" (109). Later in the novel a drunk and obnoxious Holden confronts the piano player in the bathroom of the Wicker Bar, who urges him to "Go home, Mac, like a good guy. Go home and hit the sack." An intoxicated Holden reveals the hard truth: "No home to go to. No kidding" (198). When he finally leaves the bathroom, he's crying and "feeling so damn depressed and lonesome" (198). He then wanders to an abandoned Central Park, to the pond, looking for those ducks. Perhaps they remind him of his own desire to take flight, the consequence of leaving home, or the inability to find permanence and comfort. Or perhaps Horwitz was onto something: Holden is like a fish out of water on the streets of New York, alone and—by the end of the novel—seemingly gasping for air each step he takes. yet the frozen lake, home by nature to the fish, is also incapacitating, harsh, and enclosed. "If you was a fish, Mother Nature'd take care of *you*, wouldn't she?" Horwitz argues. "You don't think them fish just die when it gets to be winter, do ya?" (109). Like any a teenager, Holden confronts the question of who will take care of him as he matures, trapped between the frightening freedom of being alone and on his own and returning to a home and family that, while providing sustenance and shelter, can be harsh, binding and cold.

Central Park, then, falls between Holden's childhood home and his forays into the adult world of New York City, geographically and emotionally. He knows the areas like the "back of [his] hand" from when he used to ride his bike and "roller-skate there all the time" (200). Yet the park at the end of his desperate night serves only to reinforce his loneliness, isolation, and deteriorating mental and physical health. Desperate to find the pond and the ducks, Holden nearly stumbles into the water, drops and breaks Phoebe's special record (an event he characterizes as "something terrible"), and begins to fear he might catch pneumonia and die from exposure. "It was just very cold and nobody around anywhere, " he tells the reader as he begins his short walk to his parent's apartment building. Although Holden is compelled to sneak into the apartment in order avoid his parents, it is very clear that he immediately finds refuge from the cold and inhospitable night. "I certainly knew I was home…Our foyer as a funny smell that doesn't smell like anyplace else. I don't know what the hell it is. It isn't cauliflower and it isn't perfume—I don't know what the hell it is—but you always know you are home" (205). These intimate sensory details contrast strongly with the unwelcome city ("vomity" smelling cabs, for instance) and his memories of Pencey (especially Ackley's ripe socks) and potently recall Holden's history of being exiled from his boyhood home and the memories that register so strongly on our senses. The theme of flight and homelessness—and the search for a refuge—continues when Phoebe figures out that Holden has once again been kicked out of school. "Daddy's gonna kill you" she cries repeatedly. Holden tries to reassure Phoebe, and himself, that he is in control:

"I'll be away," he tells her. "Ill be—I'll probably be in Colorado on this ranch."

"Don't make me laugh," she says. "You can't even ride a horse."

"Who can't? Sure I can. Certainly I can. They can teach you in about two minutes." (216).

Holden is more confident in his ability to ride a powerful animal he has probably never even touched than to negotiate the rough and tumble trails toward adulthood.

Notes

1. Like Salinger, McCarthy has provided only one major published interview in his lifetime, with Richard B. Woodward for the *New York Times Magazine*. Elements of his biography and writing life are fleshed out further by Garry Wallace's "Meeting McCarthy" in the McCarthy special issue of *Southern Quarterly* and Marty Racine's more recent biographical review for the *Houston Chronicle*. Wallace, Woodward, and Racine all confirm that McCarthy favors Melville over any other author—and all find comparisons in both his fiction and his personal life to Hemingway. According to Wallace, McCarthy compared his reluctance to meet with the press to J. D. Salinger "who had given only one interview throughout his career as a novelist, to elementary children" (135).

2. Also "All the Pretty Little Ponies," traditional, perhaps originating from slavery and the American South. See Diane Luce's discussion of the origins and possible significance of this lullaby in "When You Wake: John Grady Cole's Heroism in *All the Pretty Horses*." (156).

YASUHIRO TAKEUCHI ON THE CARNIVALESQUE

Beyond the controversy that has surrounded *The Catcher in the Rye* since it first appeared, and beyond contemporary assessments of the novel's political/cultural relevance, J. D. Salinger's *Catcher* merits ongoing consideration because of the subversion it conducts, a revolt against all fixed values. Ironically, the comment of one editor who rejected *Catcher* for publication is suggestive of the nature of this revolt: "Is Holden Caulfield suppose to be crazy?" (Hamilton 114). It is the sense of madness, often expressed in the novel through Holden's characteristic humor, that-as Mikhail Bakhtin observes in regard to carnival-"makes men look at the world with different eyes, not dimmed by 'normal,' that is by commonplace ideas and judgments" (*Rabelais* 39). This carnivalesque aspect of *Catcher* has yet to be explored fully, but it is fundamental to the novel's import and value.

In addition to madness and laughter, Bakhtin identifies other principles of the carnivalesque that offer liberation from conventional values, principles that illuminate the essential concerns of *Catcher*. These include a "peculiar festive character without any piousness, [and] complete liberation from seriousness" (*Rabelais* 254); "free and familiar contact among people": "behavior, gesture, and discourse ... freed from the authority of all hierarchical positions (social estate, rank, age, property)" (*Dostoevsky's Poetics* 123); and "disguise-that is, carnivalistic shifts of clothing and of positions and destinies in life' (125). In the spirit of the carnivalesque, Holden's story is set in the festive Christmas season, yet it is far from pious.[1] Holden himself delights in and encourages the "liberation" of a classmate who farts under his headmaster's watchful eye during the speech of a respected alumnus. During Holden's two year stay in New York, he enjoys "free and familiar contact" with diverse people, regardless of "social estate, rank, age, [and] property"; these people range from a nine-year-old girl (his sister Phoebe's friend) to a married society women in her forties (his classmate's mother), and from a prostitute to a pair of nuns. Finally, "shifts of clothing" are a recurring motif for Holden and those around him, with lendings and borrowings of his bound's-tooth jacket, his turtleneck sweater, and his famous hunting hat. How these exchanges of clothing signify shifts of "positions and destinies" shall be considered at greater length below. It is worth nothing first, however, that the received values that the novel aims to subvert encompass not merely prevailing conventions but also fundamental binary oppositions, including self/other, body/mind, father/mother, heaven/hell, life/death, writer/reader and notably, savior/saved.

This subversion of binary oppositions takes center stage at the novel's ending, the ambiguity of which has long divided *Catcher's* critics. During the final carousel scene, Holden has the following thought in reference to the children on the carousel: "If they fall off, they fall off, but it's bad if you say anything to them" (274). Holden's willingness to let his beloved sister fall has perplexed many readers because it seems to contradict his dream of becoming a "catcher in the rye"—one who saves children from falling (224). Some critics have failed even to appreciate the ambiguity resulting from this contradiction. Warren French, for instance, maintains that "Holden no longer sees himself a catcher in the rye" (121) at the novel's conclusion. Sanford Pinsker argues that "one thing is clear-Holden, the narrator, no longer clings to the same desperate scenarios that defined him as a participant in his story" (96). Underpinning such views of the novel's ending is the notion that to catch and not to catch are opposing, irreconcilable actions that cannot be taken (or aspired to) simultaneously.

Other critics have regarded the final carousel scene as less clear-cut, but have viewed its ambiguity as cause for complaint. Carl Strauch calls the novel's conclusion a "blunted, ambiguous ending" (29), and Maxwell Geismar derides it as belonging to "the New Yorker school of ambiguous finality" (198) Gerald Rosen likewise concludes that "ultimately, the problems faced by Holden ... have no 'answer' that we can hold on to" (561).

Such readings fail to appreciate that the ambiguity of the novel's ending itself provides a kind of "answer" in its blurring of the binary oppositions through which we come to understand Holden. Critics sensitive to this quality of blurring have found insight into *Catcher* in the perspective of Zen Buddhism, which, according to Zen master Daisetz Suzuski, "takes us to an absolute realm wherein there are no antitheses of any sort" (68). In their pioneering study "Zen and Salinger," Bernice and Sanford Goldstein observe Holden's Zen-like identification with the very people he criticizes, as well as the underlying unity ("wherein there are no antitheses") reflected in the catcher Holden's being caught by both Phoebe and his deceased younger brother Allie (322).[2] Dennis McCort extends this perspective by considering the specific influence of Suzuki on Salinger, maintaining that in the carousel scene, Holden transcends the "contradiction between permanence and change" (266). In the readings of these critics, Zen Buddhism affords substantial insight into the ambivalence of Catcher's conclusion. Yet the Zen approach to Catcher is less successful in explaining the novel's blasphemous, carnivalesque aspect. In concluding that Holden "is caught by love" (322), for instance, the Goldsteins privilege a static principle (love/hate) that, in a larger sense, Catcher overturns[3]—a typical reversal of binary oppositions upon which Bakhtin, perhaps, casts a clearer light than Zen.

(...)

The Identity Between the Hunter and His Prey

Salinger's catcher-related imagery is paradoxical: Holden is both savior and saved; Holden's younger siblings Phoebe and Allie, as shall be shown, represent the caught even as they act to catch Holden. The image of Jesus Christ that Jung develops in *Aion* embodies a similar paradox, and will prove helpful to a discussion of the identity between the savior and the saved in *Catcher*. [6]

Jung considers Christ as being both fisherman and fish, remarking that "the Christian Ichthys is a fisher of men par excellence" (*Aion* 112). Jung observes that as "Christ wants to make Peter and Andrew 'fishers of men, and as "miraculous draught of fishes (Luke 5:10) is used by Christ ... as a paradigm for Peter's missionary activity" (89). Jesus is himself a fisher of men. Yet as Jung notes, the fish has become a universal symbol of Jesus Christ because "*Ichthys*" or "*Ichthus*." an abbreviation of "Iesous Christos Theou Uios Soter" (Greek for "Jesus Christ Son of God Savior"), means "fish" (Fish"). Jung's conception of the identity between the hunter and his prey" (112) thus poses a challenge to conventional notions of the hunter (savior) and the prey (saved) as existing in an overdetermined hierarchical relationship.

Salinger explores a similar conception of the hunter (savior)/prey (saved) relationship through similar imagery. In his later story, "Seymour: An Introduction," narrator Buddy Glass refers to the unity of fisherman and fish directly:

> The hazards of fishing in general were themselves a favorite subject to Seymour's. Our younger brother Walt was a great bent-pin fisherman as a small boy, and for his ninth or tenth birthday he received a poem from Seymour-one of the major delights of his life, I believe-about a little rich boy who catches a Lafayette in the Hudson River, experiences a fierce pain in his own lower lip on reeling him in, then dismissed the matter from his mind, only to discover when he is home and the still-alive fish has been given the run of the bathtub that he, the fish, is wearing a blue serge cap with the same school insignia over the peak as the boy's own; the boy finds his own name-tape sewn inside the tine we cap. (143-44).

Clearly, the fisher boy has caught himself as prey. Considering the fish as a symbol of Jesus Christ, the two identical caps in Seymour's poem not only suggest the identity of savior and saved, but also bring to mind the case of Holden Caulfield in particular, who as savior/catcher, wears a hat-the red hunting cap that he both gives to and has returned by Phoebe (exchanges to be considered in detail below).

In light of the cap in Seymour's poem, the significance of Holden's calling his cap "a people shooting hat" is clear. If the hat were "a deer shooting hat, " as Holden's dormitory neighbor Ackley suggests, it would represent the conventional binary opposition of hunter and prey. However, Holden firmly states that"[1] this is a people shooting hat ... I shoot people in this hat (30), an assertion that resonates with the Jungian identity of hunter (savior)/prey (saved). Furthermore, although Holden's cap confers a hunter identity, Holden often imagines himself as a wounded, suffering gunshot victim (135,195). Holden is thus at once the shooter and the shot, an ambivalent hunter akin to Jung's fisherman, Jesus.

The nature of "catching" in the novel lends nuance to its representation of "the identity between the hunter and his prey." Imagining a catcher in the rye, Holden dreams of preventing children from falling off a cliff, a notion of catching that presupposes the conventional binary opposition of life and death, in which case life is preferable to death. But Holden's dream (like this conventional notion of the life/death opposition) is informed by the many acts of picking up the fallen-as opposed to catching the falling-that occur throughout the novel.[7]

A particularly resonant instance of picking up concerns a phonograph record that Holden buys as a present for Phoebe but drops and breaks before giving to her. The fictional song on this record, "Little Shirley Beans," concerns a girl who has lost two of her front teeth. Considered in light of *Catcher's* Christmas setting, this song is surely patterned on the 1949 hit, "All I Want For Christmas (Is My Two Front Teeth)," sung by Spike Jones and His City Slickers. This real song tells us how the little girl lost her teeth: she "slid down the banister just as fast as ... [she] could" (Jones), and was injured. Like the fictional fallen record, the girl in the real song falls and is not caught. Given this parallel, it follows that the broken pieces of the record can be understood to represent the fallen. Significantly, Holden picks up these pieces and gives them to Phoebe despite their condition. Phoebe responds, "I'm *saving* them" (212, emphasis added); the fallen girl can be understood to merit the same treatment: to be picked up and saved.

Notes

1. For example, Holden finds it amusing to hear a Christmas tree called "sonuvabitch" (255), and finds absurd "this Christmas thing [performance] they have at Radio City, "of which he observes, "[O]ld Jesus probably would've puked if He could see it" (178).

2. Though less concerned with Zen Buddhism, Clinton Trowbridge argues along similar lines in observing that Holden himself is a phony because he often recognized images of himself in

those of phony people. See Trowbridge, "Character and Detail" 74-79, and "Symbolic Structure" 691-92.

3. For a view similar to Goldstein's, see also Trowbridge 78. Without specific reference to Zen, critics including John M. Howell and Jonathan Baumbach have also suggested that Holden is saved by the love of his younger siblings. See Howell 375, and Baumbach 472.

6. *Aion* was originally published in Germany in 1947. An English version was published in 1951, the year of *Catcher's* publication.

7. To offer several examples, Holden's teacher, Mr. Spencer, drops a piece of chalk that a student picks up (10), and drops a magazine and an exam paper that Holden picks up (14, 17) Holden later picks up the straw basket of one of the nuns he meets (142).

Works by J.D. Salinger

The Catcher in the Rye, 1951.

Nine Stories, 1953; republished as *For Esmé—With Love and Squalor, and Other Stories*, 1953.

Raise High the Roof Beam, Carpenters and Seymour: An Introduction, 1959.

Franny and Zooey, 1961.

"Hapworth 16, 1924," 1965.

The Complete Uncollected Short Stories of J.D. Salinger, 1974.

Annoted Bibliography

Alexander, Paul. "Inventing Holden Caulfield." From *Salinger: A Biography*. Los Angeles: Renaissance Books (1999): 63–77.

From an important biography of J.D. Salinger, this chapter traces the author's thoughts on his writing as well as the momentous political events and personal aspirations in 1940-41. Alexander discusses the short stories Salinger published during this interval and identifies the two most important ones which were the imaginative foundation for Holden's character in *The Catcher in the Rye*. The first story, "The Young Folks," which gained Salinger entry into the highly desirable and prestigious *New Yorker*, is a story about rich, jaded teenagers from New York, most especially its very animated, yet neurotic, teenage protagonist from the Upper East Side, named Holden Caulfield. The second story, "Slight Rebellion Off Madison," continues the saga of the privileged teenager, Holden Caulfield, who makes a drunken confession to his girlfriend, Sally Hayes, that he is very unhappy with his privileged lifestyle.

Baumbach, Jonathan. "The Saint as a Young Man: A Reappraisal of *The Catcher in the Rye*." From *Modern Language Quarterly*, vol XXV, no. 4 (December 1964): 461–72.

Here Baumbach posits an interpretation for the world of *The Catcher in the Rye* in which innocence, which is "Holden's fantasy-vision" and his selfless desire to protect children leaves him with only two options, either insanity or "sainthood," with Holden wishing for the latter. Baumbach sees Holden as an aspiring "saint" in desperate need of an exemplary role model, which desperation forms the crux of his problem, namely the absence of a spiritual father. Citing the failures of such men as Spencer and Antolini, who leave Holden to suffer for the conscience of an evil world and utterly incapable of redeeming it, Baumbach nevertheless sees hope and blessing in the love he has for his younger sister, Phoebe, and his deceased brother Allie.

Brookman, Christopher. "Pencey Preppy: Cultural Codes in *The Catcher in the Rye*." From *New Essays on The Catcher in the Rye*. Edited by Jack Salzman. New York: Cambridge University Press (1991): 57–76.

In this essay Bookerman emphasizes the critical role played by the American prep school as the most important instrument of social control. Discusses the evolution of the prep school from the nineteenth century forward, and sees Salinger as relying on two factors in his portrayal of Pencey Prep—first, Holden's debunking assessments of its traditions and customs and, second, his ritualistic encounters with both his peers and the Pencey hierarchy. Slabey argues that Holden is both victim and exploiter of the system in which he lives.

Bryan, James. "The Psychological Structure of *The Catcher in the Rye*." From *PMLA* 89, no, 5 (October 1974): 1065–74. © 1974 by The Modern Language Association of America.

Bryan's essay begins with the premise that many critics have overlooked Holden Caulfield's immaturity who, among other problems, suffers from a hypersensitivity which is neurotically induced. Bryan identifies a pattern in Holden's experiences whereby he sets himself up for failure. Ultimately, however, Bryan maintains that he does finally achieve maturity.

Cohen, Hubert I. "'A Woeful Agony which Forced Me to Begin My Tale': *The Catcher in the Rye*." From *Modern Fiction Studies*, vol. XII, no. 3 (Autumn 1966): 355–66.

Cohen conceives of Holden as a self-conscious writer whose motive for telling his story is therapeutic. Focusing on what he finds to be Holden's ultimate dilemma, namely his inability to find help from the people he knows, Cohen maintains that Holden's ultimate resolution of this crisis is to appeal to his readers for help in explaining his story to him. This public plea for help, according to Cohen, involves the art of storytelling, a skill in which Holden takes great pride, from the very beginning in which he tells us he has thought about how he will tell his story to the very end in which he warns the reader against pursuing an activity from which he himself will not desist - the analysis of what is wrong with him and the world he inhabits. Cohen concludes that Holden's choice to continue pursuing answers for the sake of his own sanity is also Salinger's message about the painful process an artist must endure for the sake of his art.

Edwards, Duane. "Holden Caulfield: 'Don't Ever Tell Anybody Anything.'" From *English Literary History (ELH)* vol. 44, no. 3 (Fall 1977): 554–65.

Duane's piece challenges those critics who idealize Holden as an anti-establishment figure by arguing that his dominant character trait is ambivalence, an indication of mental instability. Edwards reads Holden as a hypocrite who actively participates in the very phoniness he protests against, rather than the values he seems to espouse. He sees Holden as retreating from, rather than accepting, the challenges of the world he inhabits. In sum, Edwards interprets Holden's character as that of an unreliable narrator who will never be able to assume responsibility for his own actions or be able to save others.

Evertson, Matt. "Love, Loss, and Growing Up in J.D. Salinger and Cormac McCarthy." From *The Catcher in the Rye: New Essays*. New York: Peter Lang Publishing Inc. (2002): 101–41.

This essay sets forth the similarities in character between Holden Caulfield and John Grady, the protagonist of *All the Pretty Horses*, both of which novels concern the same historical time period and the attendant problems of "coming of age" in post World War II America. Evertson organizes his essay around three fundamental issues that resonate with teenagers in each novel: the choice and control that adolescents yearn for; an exploration of the problems that accompany the attempts to control the processes of time and maturation; and, finally, a treatment of the larger, cosmic themes of love and death that make these novels essential to the American canon.

French, Warren. "The Artist as a Very Nervous Young Man." From *J.D. Salinger*. Boston: G.K. Hall & Co. (1976): 102–29. © 1976 by G.K. Hall & Co.

French analyzes Holden Caulfield's character as that of an emerging young artist struggling with the attendant emotional and physical problems that beset that vocation. As further support for this paradigm, French maintains that the popularity of the novel with fully literate youth, as well as their easy identification with Holden, is attributable to the fact that Holden seeks sympathy and understanding during a very difficult period in his life. French maintains that the major thrust of the novel is his quest for tranquility and compassion, and concludes that Holden has developed intellectually by acquiring the particular knowledge shared by other artists—an insight into the difficulties and challenges that such a profession involves.

Howell, John M. "Salinger in the Waste Land." From *Modern Fiction Studies*, vol. XII, no. 3 (Autumn 1966): 367–75.

Howell's piece discusses the influence of *The Wasteland* on *Catcher in the Rye*, identifying various parallels structures in Eliot to be found in Salinger's novel—the burial of the dead in which Holden's farewell to old Spencer resembles Madame Sosotris whose fortune-telling Tarot cards are associated with ancient Egypt, the same topic Holden wrote on and whose poor performance elicits a dismal prognosis from his former teacher; the game of checkers in which Jane Gallagher resembles Eliot's lady who displays both fear and lust as she plays the game, and, finally, resemblance to the

Grail Knight's entry into the Perilous Chapel and Cemetery in *The Waste Land* in several instance such as his calling out to his deceased brother Allie across a terrifying abyss.

Lee, A. Robert. "Flunking Everything Else Except English Anyway: Holden Caulfield, Author." From *Critical Essays on Salinger's The Catcher in the Rye*. Edited by Joel Salzberg. Boston: G.K. Hall & Co. (1990): 226–37. © 1990 by Joel Salzberg.

This essay focuses on "composition" as the key term in the novel as it applies to Holden Caulfield's consummate artistry in forever composing new themes and identities for himself, creating a fictional autobiography which is, at the same time, accompanied by an overwhelming anxiety of disappearing. Lee maintains that Holden's abject fear of becoming invisible is either erased or overcome in the process of transforming it from reality into a skillfully fashioned narrative and, finally, it is Holden's gift for storytelling that evidences his path to psychological health and his eventual inclusion in the community of authors and artists who have "made over the world on their own creative terms."

Miller, Edwin Haviland. "In Memoriam: Allie Caulfield in *The Catcher in the Rye*." From *Mosaic* 15, no. 1 (Winter 1982): 129–140. © 1982 by *Mosaic*.

Miller's essay sees Holden Caulfield's emotional problems as an inability to mourn his brother Allie in terms of both his anger and his guilt. Miller provides a very thorough and persuasive psychoanalysis of Holden's alienation from all with whom he comes in contact, citing numerous instances in which Holden provokes hostility and/or orchestrates his own failure. Yet, all of Holden's emotional problems notwithstanding, Miller sees Holden as having achieved maturity and transcendence in the final chapter as evidenced by his acceptance of life as a carousel ride that goes round and round without definitive answers.

Pinsker, Sanford. *The Catcher in the Rye: Innocence Under Pressure*. New York: Twayne Publishers, 1993.

Pinsker's volume begins with a very helpful discussion of the historical and literary context of *Catcher in the Rye* as well as an overview of its critical reception. This is followed by a reading of the novel in which Pinsker retropes Ernest Hemingway's "grace under pressure" to characterize Holden Caulfield's struggle against a world of hypocrisy and corruption. Pinsker's reading is divided into four separate crises: Holden's expulsion from Pencey Prep; his dangerous odyssey during his stay in a Manhattan hotel; his futile, and at times traumatic, attempts to communicate with various people whom he used to respect; and the conclusion of his madman weekend when he is reunited with his beloved younger sister, Phoebe, who points out the absurdity of his dream of escaping civilization.

Rosen, Gerald. "A Retrospective Look at *The Catcher in the Rye*." From *American Quarterly*, vol. XXIX, no. 5 (Winter 1977): 547–51.

This essay maintains that *Catcher in the Rye* is basically a novel of disillusionment and interprets Holden Caulfield's experiences as a parallel to the life of Buddha, both of whom were born to a privileged life which is radically transformed when they encounter old age, sickness and death and both of whom resolve to leave their sheltered surroundings in search of a spiritual guide to help them come to terms with these. Rosen maintains that for Holden, the turning point occurs when he encounters Phoebe at his parents' apartment, as she is the one who truly sees and cannot be lied to. Ultimately, Phoebe is the one who enables Holden to turn away from obsessive grieving for his deceased brother Allie and instead find happiness in recognizing what he still has in the present.

Rowe, Joyce. "Holden Caulfield and American Protest." From *New Essays on The Catcher in the Rye*. Edited by Jack Salzman. New York: Cambridge University Press (1991): 77–95. © 1991 by Cambridge University Press.

Rowe's essay reads *Catcher in the Rye* as a demonstration of Salinger's ability to infuse the conventional representation of a disaffected and tormented adolescent with a historical resonance within the context of earlier American writers who grappled with the displacement of the individual in a morally corrupt society. Rowe contrasts Holden, who is born into a postwar culture devoid of respect for humanity and utterly without hope as standing in stark contrast to such writers as Thoreau who believed that the promise of a renewed society resided in the spiritual regeneration of the individual. Nevertheless, Rowe maintains that Holden shares a common character trait with his literary forebears, namely a resistance to questioning the ambivalences of his own nature, thereby rendering him powerless to engage the world and that the complaint made by some critics that Holden offers no substitute for the world at which he rages is exactly the point.

Shaw, Peter. "Love and Death in *The Catcher in the Rye*." From *New Essays on The Catcher in the Rye*. Edited by Jack Salzman. New York: Cambridge University Press (1991): 97–114

Shaw's essay reads Holden's personality as an individual psychological case, rather than a familiar character in the American novel of "the sensitive youth beleaguered by society. Shaw maintains that Holden Caulfield's critique of society is neither universally endorsed nor does the end of his narrative represent a capitulation to society as the culture of the 1950's may have believed. Instead, he focuses on the universal themes of love and death as they specifically relate to critical events in the novel. Among the many details of Holden's individual experiences, Shaw cites his response to two separate museum exhibits—first, his visit to the Museum of Natural History in which the Indian and his squaw will always remain unchanged and in the same serene relationship to one another, unlike his parents and, second, his visit to the Metropolitan Museum of Art in which he leads two small but frightened boys to the mummies, only to be left alone in peaceful contemplation with eternal death, and which contemplation brings up wishes to preserve his beloved, deceased brother Allie.

Slabey, Robert M. "*The Catcher in the Rye*: Christian Theme and Symbol." From *CLA Journal*, vol. VI, no. 3 (March 1963): 170–83.

Slabey offers a reading of *The Catcher in the Rye* as a Christian novel, premised on the fact that it takes place during Advent ..... (p. 172). Slabey interprets the world of Catcher as evidencing a desperate need for redemption with Holden Caulfield, a highly sympathetic character who loves children and worries about the ducks in Central Park as a young man in need of redemption himself before he can help others. Slabey argues that Catcher has a positive ending in that Holden's ability to forgive those who have wronged him, including Stradlater, Ackley and the very evil Maurice, is a sign that he is emerging from the depths of his own loneliness and alienation.

Strauch, Carl F. "Kings in the Back Row: Meaning Through Structure—A Reading of Salinger's *The Catcher in the Rye*." From *Wisconsin Studies in Contemporary Literature* vol. 2, no. 1 (Winter 1961): 5–30.

Strauch argues that the critics of *The Catcher in the Rye* have thus far missed a crucial point—namely, that as a work of art it is a complex novel in terms of structure, language, episode and character—the appreciation of which will reveal a highly wrought psychological drama of unremitting terror and ultimate beauty. He maintains that by the novel's conclusion,

Holden Caulfield emerges triumphant. According to Strauch, Holden's success is the result of his having matured and, in so doing, brought about his own cure in transcending the social and institutional chaos that surrounds him.

Steinle, Pamela Hunt. *In Cold Fear: The Catcher in the Rye: Censorship Controversies and Postwar American Character.* Columbus: Ohio State University Press, 2000.

Hunt's volume interprets the novel as a metaphor of the American process of maturity in the Cold War era whereby the innocent and idealistic childhood is replaced by an adult middle-class which unquestioningly accepts the pursuit of status and power as its desired goal. Provides an excellent overview of the critical debate, most especially a discussion of the transformation of the myth of the an earlier American Adam confident in his ability to shape his own destiny to Salinger's protagonist who must struggle against hopelessness and alienation. Steinle posits a hopeful conclusion with Holden Caulfield emerging with a strong sense of self and the ways in which he differs from those who choose to conform.

Takeuchi, Yasuhiro. "The Burning Carousel and the Carnivalesque: Subversion and Transcendence at the Close of *The Catcher in the Rye*." From *Studies in the Novel*, vol. XXXIV, no. 3 (Fall 2002): 320–36.

Takeuchi applies Bakhtin's concept of the carnivalesque, a world turned upside down in which conventional values and social norms are overturned, to the climactic scene when Phoebe rides the carousel in Central Park. Takeuchi maintains that this is the critical moment when Holden, who endures a drenching rain while everyone else runs for shelter, is finally able to transcend his desire to reenact Allie's tragic death and, instead, replaces his brother. The rain becomes the vehicle for a blessing from Allie thereby enabling Holden to realize his dream of becoming the catcher. To this paradigm of the carnivalesque, Takeuchi adds the mediating influence of Zen Buddhism and Jungian psychology, both of which systems resolve the dilemmas and ambiguities of events in the novel.

Contributors

Harold Bloom is Sterling Professor of the Humanities at Yale University. He is the author of 30 books, including *Shelley's Mythmaking* (1959), *The Visionary Company* (1961), *Blake's Apocalypse* (1963), *Yeats* (1970), *A Map of Misreading* (1975), *Kabbalah and Criticism* (1975), *Agon: Toward a Theory of Revisionism* (1982), *The American Religion* (1992), *The Western Canon* (1994), and *Omens of Millennium: The Gnosis of Angels, Dreams, and Resurrection* (1996). *The Anxiety of Influence* (1973) sets forth Professor Bloom's provocative theory of the literary relationships between the great writers and their predecessors. His most recent books include *Shakespeare: The Invention of the Human* (1998), a 1998 National Book Award finalist, *How to Read and Why* (2000), *Genius: A Mosaic of One Hundred Exemplary Creative Minds* (2002), *Hamlet: Poem Unlimited* (2003), *Where Shall Wisdom Be Found?* (2004), and *Jesus and Yahweh: The Names Divine* (2005). In 1999, Professor Bloom received the prestigious American Academy of Arts and Letters Gold Medal for Criticism. He has also received the International Prize of Catalonia, the Alfonso Reyes Prize of Mexico, and the Hans Christian Andersen Bicentennial Prize of Denmark.

Janyce Marson is a doctoral student at New York University. She is working on a doctoral dissertation on the rhetoric of the mechanical in Coleridge, Wordsworth and Mary Shelley.

Carl F. Strauch (1908–1989) was Professor of English at Lehigh University. He is the editor of and author of "Emerson Rejects Reed and Hails Thoreau" (1968); "The Sources of Emerson's 'Song of Nature'" (1955); and editor of *Style in the American Renaissance: A Symposium* (1970).

Robert M. Slabey was Professor Emeritus of English at the University of Notre Dame. He is the author "Diminished Bodies and American War Literature" (1998); "Carson

McCuller's Allegory of Love" (1993) and "Quentin Compson's 'Lost Childhood'" (1964).

Jonathan Baumbach has been a Professor of English at Brooklyn College, the City University of New York. He is the author of *B: A Novel* (2002); *Separate Hours: A Novel* (1990); and *The Landscape of Nightmare: Studies in the Contemporary American Novel* (1965).

John M. Howell is Professor Emeritus at Southern Illinois University-Carbondale. He is the author of "Hemingway and Chaplin: Monkey Business in 'The Undefeated'" (1990); *Understanding John Gardner* (1993); and "Faulkner, Prufrock, and Agamemnon: Horses, Hell, and High Water" (1980).

Warren French is the author of "Steinbeck's 'Self-characters' as 1930s Underdogs" (2002); *John Steinbeck's Nonfiction Revisited* (1996); *The San Francisco Poetry Renaissance, 1955–1960* (1991); and *Jack Kerouac* (1986).

Duane Edwards has been Professor of English at Fairleigh Dickinson University. He is the author of *The Rainbow: A Search for New Life* (1990); "Erich Neumann and the Shadow Problem in *The Plumed Serpent*" (1991); and "The Problem of Narcissism in Lawrence's Late Fiction" (1993–1994).

Gerald Rosen is Professor Emeritus of Creative Writing at Sonoma State University. He is the author of *Zen and the Art of J.D. Salinger* (1977) and *Mahatma Gandhi in a Cadillac* (1995).

Edwin Haviland Miller is Professor Emeritus at New York University. He is the author of *Salem is My Dwelling Place: A life of Nathaniel Hawthorne* (1991); *Walt Whitman's "Song of Myself": A Mosaic of Interpretations* (1989); and *Melville* (1975) and editor of the six-volume *Correspondence of Walt Whitman* (1961–77).

Christopher Brookeman has been a lecturer in American Studies at the University of Westminster. He is the author of *American Culture and Society Since the 1930s* (1984).

Sandford Pinsker has been a Professor of Humanities at Franklin and Marshall College in Lancaster, Pennyslvania. He is the author of "Saul Bellow's Herzog" (2004); "Leslie Fiedler 1917–2003" (2003); and *Bearing the Bad News: Contemporary American Literature and Culture* (1990).

Paul Alexander is the author of *Rough Magic: A Biography of Sylvia Plath* (1991); *Boulevard of Broken Dreams: The Life, Times, and Legend of James Dean* (1994); and editor of *Ariel Ascending: Writings about Sylvia Plath* (1985).

Pamela Hunt Steinle is a Graduate Director and Professor of American Studies at California State University, Fullerton. She is the author of "The Art of Viewing Off-Center: Television and the Intellectual Enterprise" (1998) and serves on the national Advisory Board of the Iowa Journal of Cultural Studies

Matt Evertson has been a Professor in the Department of Language and Literature Chadron State College. He is the author of "'Stephen Crane and 'Some Others'" (2001).

Yasuhiro Takeuchi is the author of "Resistance and Japanese Literature" (1972) and "The National Liberation Struggle as Reflected in Japanese Literature" (1970).

Acknowledgments

Strauch, Carl F. "Kings in the Back Row: Meaning Through Structure—A Reading of Salinger's *The Catcher in the Rye*." From *Wisconsin Studies in Contemporary Literature* vol. 2, no. 1 (Winter 1961): 6–9 and 29.

Slabey, Robert M. "*The Catcher in the Rye*: Christian Theme and Symbol." From *CLA Journal* vol. VI, no. 3 (March 1963): 170–173. © 1963 by The College Language Association. Reprinted by permission.

Baumbach, Jonathan. "The Saint as a Young Man: A Reappraisal of The Catcher in the Rye." From Modern Language Quarterly vol. XXV, no. 4 (December 1964): 461–464. © 1964 by Duke University Press. Reprinted by permission.

Howell, John M. "Salinger in the Waste Land." From *Modern Fiction Studies* vol. XII, no. 3 (Autumn 1966): 367–371. © 1966 by the Purdue Research Foundation. Reprinted by permission.

French, Warren. "The Artist as a Very Nervous Young Man." From *J.D. Salinger*. Boston: G.K. Hall & Co. (1976): 107–111. © 1976 by G.K. Hall & Co. Reprinted by permission.

Edwards, Duane. "Holden Caulfield: "Don't Ever Tell Anybody Anything." From *English Literary History* 44, no. 3 (Fall 1977): 554–557. © 1977 by The Johns Hopkins University Press. Reprinted by permission.

Rosen, Gerald. "A Retrospective Look at *The Catcher in the Rye*." From *American Quarterly*, vol. XXIX, no. 5 (Winter 1977): 547–551. © 1977 by the Trustees of the University of Pennsylvania. Reprinted by permission.

Miller, Edwin Haviland. "*In Memoriam: Allie Caulfield in* The Catcher in the Rye." From *Mosaic* 15, no. 1 (Winter 1982): 129–132. © 1982 by Mosaic. Reprinted by permission.

Brookeman, Christopher. "Pencey Preppy: Cultural Codes in *The Catcher in the Rye.*" From *New Essays on The Catcher in the Rye.* Edited by Jack Salzman. New York: Cambridge University Press (1991): 58–63.

Pinsker, Sanford. "O Pencey, My Pencey!" From *The Catcher in the Rye: Innocence Under Pressure.* New York, N.Y.: Twayne Publishers (1993): 28–31. © 1993 by Twayne Publishers. Reprinted by permission.

Alexander, Paul. "Inventing Holden Caulfield." From *Salinger: A Biography.* Los Angeles: Renaissance Books (1999): 74–77. © 1999 by Paul Alexander. Reprinted by permission.

Steinle, Pamela Hunt. "The Catcher in the Rye as *Postwar American Fable.*" From *In Cold Fear: The Catcher in the Rye: Censorship Controversies and Postwar American Character.* Columbus: Ohio State University Press (2000): 20–23. © 2000 by The Ohio State University. Reprinted by permission.

Evertson, Matt. "Lover, Loss, and Growing Up in J.D. Salinger and Cormac McCarthy. From *The Catcher in the Rye: New Essays.* New York: Peter Lang (2002): 101–102 and 104-7. © 2002 by Peter Lang Publishing, Inc. Reprinted by permission.

Takeuchi, Yasuhiro. "The Burning Carousel and the Carnivalesque: Subversion and Transcendence at the Close of *The Catcher in the Rye.*" From *Studies in the Novel,* vol. XXXIV, no. 3 (Fall 2002): 320–324. © 2002 by the University of North Texas. Reprinted by permission.

Index